Autism, Advocates, and Law Enforcement Professionals

of related interest

Asperger's Syndrome
A Guide for Parents and Professionals
Tony Attwood
ISBN 1 85302 577 1

A Positive Approach to Autism
Stella Waterhouse
ISBN 1 85302 808 8

Asperger Syndrome Employment Workbook
An Employment Workbook for Adults with Asperger Syndrome
Roger N. Meyer
ISBN 1 85302 796 0

Pretending to be Normal
Living with Asperger's Syndrome
Liane Holliday Willey
ISBN 1 85302 749 9

Breaking Autism's Barriers
A Father's Story
Bill Davis, as told to Wendy Goldband Schunick
ISBN 1 85302 979 3

Through the Eyes of Aliens
A Book About Autistic People
Jasmine Lee O'Neill
ISBN 1 85302 710 0

Hitchhiking Through Asperger Syndrome
Lise Pyles
ISBN 1 85302 937 8

Autistic Thinking – This is the Title
Peter Vermeulen
ISBN 1 85302 995 5

Autism, Advocates, and Law Enforcement Professionals

Recognizing and Reducing Risk Situations for People with Autism Spectrum Disorders

Dennis Debbaudt

Jessica Kingsley Publishers
London and Philadelphia

The right of Dennis Debbaudt to be identified as author of this work has been asserted by him in accordance with the Copyright, Designs and Patents Act 1988.

First published in the United Kingdom in 2002 by
Jessica Kingsley Publishers Ltd,
116 Pentonville Road, London
N1 9JB, England
and
325 Chestnut Street,
Philadelphia PA 19106, USA.

www.jkp.com

Library of Congress Cataloging in Publication Data
A CIP catalog record for this book is available from the Library of Congress

British Library Cataloguing in Publication Data
A CIP catalogue record for this book is available from the British Library

ISBN 1 85302 980 7

Printed and Bound in Great Britain by
Athenaeum Press, Gateshead, Tyne and Wear

To those in law enforcement:
You have the toughest job in the world.

To the children and adults with autism:
I hope this helps others understand.

To my wife, Gay, and my son, Kelly:
Thank you for allowing me to write this book.

To my mother, Evelyn, and my father, Eugene:
I know you would be very proud.

Contents

Section Two

THE CITIZEN'S PERSPECTIVE

Acknowledgments

I want to acknowledge those who offered their time, suggestions, advice, and assistance in the preparation of this book: Margaret Creedon, Ph.D.; Gene Debbaudt, retired Special Agent of the Federal Bureau of Investigation; Peter Gerhardt, Ed. D.; Jean Haase; Pat Hawk; Andrew Maltz, Ph.D.; Darla Rothman, Ph.D.; Jeff Sell; Art Wallen, M.S.; Mary Weisenfeld, R.N., C.E.N.; and, especially, Ellen Kerfoot, R.N., B.S.

I also want to thank the people with autism, their families, and professionals in autism and law enforcement who have shared their personal stories and offered support for my work over the past ten years. I deeply appreciate it and believe that telling others about your stories makes a difference. Let each one, reach one.

SECTION ONE

The Law Enforcement
Perspective

1

Introduction

As Police Officer Shari Lohman patrolled her beat on the afternoon of 21 April, 1985, she noted a teenaged boy on a beach-cruiser bicycle riding ahead of her on the road. Though there was nothing initially suspicious about the young man, the officer's instincts were aroused when she observed the teen look over his shoulder at her patrol car, then jump off the seat of his bike and start to run while pushing the bike. When the officer stopped her patrol car and got out, the young man jumped back on the bike and pedaled away.

Now believing that the teen was riding a stolen bike, Officer Lohman got back into her patrol car and began a slow pursuit. She called out on the car's loudspeaker for the biker to stop, but the teenager continued to pedal away. At this point, the policewoman radioed her dispatcher and asked for assistance.

Nearby, Sergeant Jim Lowder heard the call, joined the pursuit, and saw the teen biker through the windows of his patrol car. When the teen saw Sgt. Lowder leave his vehicle and approach him, he dropped from his bike and began running. By this display of behavior, Lowder now believed that the teen might be under the influence of a hallucinogenic drug, possibly phencyclidine, a drug known on the streets as PCP.

Lowder and another officer, David Stoermer, who joined in the chase, now pursued the teenager. The young man then ran into a garage, the officers close behind. The police, wanting to capture the suspect before he could enter a place where weapons, accomplices, or victims might be, forcibly subdued the teenager.

It was at this point that the officers learned from neighbors and the boy's mother that the young man, Guido Rodriguez Jr., had autism, that the bike he rode was his own, and that the garage he had entered was part of his family's home.

What had seemed a routine police chase became a very regrettable incident and quickly escalated into a tragedy when it was learned that Guido was suffering from considerable pain due to injuries sustained in the struggle to subdue him. One of his kidneys had been damaged, was hemorrhaging, and had to be surgically removed. Subsequently, a $10 million damage claim was filed against the city of Irvine, California, its police department, and the three officers.

This needless tragedy occurred because the officers involved did not know that Guido had autism. They didn't understand that innocent Guido, whose autism left him with little usable speech and without the ability to understand or respond to the officers that day, was only trying to get to the safe haven where he was understood and accepted. The officers did not know that a person with autism might, when confronted, display suspicious or inappropriate behaviors. They did not know that persons with autism may be unresponsive, that they often run from the police or others they perceive as strangers. The officers did not know that people like Guido might respond inappropriately to loud noises, like the sound of a voice through a loudspeaker. In a way, the police were as handicapped as Guido that day. Autism awareness had not been part of their training.

Yet the Irvine Police Department saw to it that some good came out of this very negative incident. The department recognized that the only way to avoid such incidents in the future was to change either the behavior of people with autism or the behavior of the police. With the help of advocates and experts, they resolved to do both.

The result of their resolve is Operation Mainstream, a program dedicated to improving the interactions between law enforcers and children with autism and other developmental disabilities. These young people are given opportunities to become familiar with police officers as members of their community, to be part of mock interviews, and to learn how to respond appropriately to basic informational questions like giving their names, where they live, what their phone numbers are, or if they have identification cards. At the same time, the police officers get to see first hand just how these children act; they begin to see the differences between various disabilities and degrees of similar disabilities. As they interact with the children, they begin to develop the sensitivity and skills needed to deal effectively with developmentally disabled people they may encounter in field situations.

Positive developments can take place when the law enforcement and autism communities collaborate to share information that helps police officers better understand the behavior of people they encounter in field situations, and helps children and adults with autism to become equipped to identify, understand, and react appropriately with police officers.

This book takes a look at the current information available about the interactions between law enforcement professionals and people with autism. It addresses issues important to law enforcers, advocates, and persons with autism, and offers some solutions. Identifying and resolving the problems that those with autism present to law enforcement professionals will always be a work in progress. But it is grounded in the belief that basic improvements that lead to more positive community experiences for all concerned can be accomplished when we acknowledge the root solution: better recognition of and response to the basic needs of people with autism and law enforcement professionals.

2

Autism Recognition and Response

What is autism?

Recognition and response is the key for law enforcement professionals to understand the needs of the rising autistic population. Most importantly, law enforcers need to recognize the signs of autism in order to provide for the welfare and safety of all citizens and avoid needless litigation. But just what is autism?

Autism is a neurologically based developmental disability that seriously affects a person's communication, socialization, and decision-making skills. Typically noticed in children by age three years, it affects males four times more than females. It is conservatively estimated to occur in at least 12 million people globally, without respect to racial or ethnic background. The incidence of autism is sharply on the rise. In the late 1980's, autism was reported to occur in 2–5 persons per 10,000. In 2001, the rate of occurrence is reported in some areas of the United States at 1 in every 250 persons.

There is no known cure for autism, although medication may help some of the symptoms in some cases. There are often great efforts made by parents and educators to help children with autism change their behaviors, making it easier for them to assimilate into a social world. Research into genetic and environmental markers continues, but its causes remain unknown. At one time, autism was thought to be caused by the way parents raised their children. However, we now know that autism is biologically determined and that it is a lifelong disability. Early diagnosis and access to educational programs offer the best hope for those affected.

The terms autism and Autism Spectrum Disorder (ASD) are those that will be used in this book. However, it is worth noting that there are many different terms that one may hear that are included within the broader category of ASDs. Such terms as: Asperger's Syndrome; Rett's Syndrome; Pervasive Developmental Delay – Not Otherwise Specified (PDD-NOS); Heller's Syndrome, also known as Childhood Disintegrative Disorder (CDD); and Landau-Kleffner Syndrome (LKS), also called Acquired Aphasia with Epilepsy, are all terms for conditions that can look similar to autism. Each of these conditions has its specific symptoms and characteristics, but for purposes here it is enough to recognize them as coming under the umbrella category of ASD.

Autism is a complex disorder that includes multiple levels of functioning, from mild to severe. Among individuals with autism, level of functioning usually pertains to cognitive levels with a range from severe mental retardation to superior abilities. While cognitive ability will have a significant effect on whether a person with autism will be verbal or nonverbal and whether he or she will function with greater degrees of independence, all persons with autism have significant problems responding appropriately in social environments.

The combination of different levels of functioning, varied patterns, and unusual response of people with autism, presents a serious challenge to law enforcers, who we know are encountering individuals with autism every day.

Autism is defined by the presence of certain behaviors. Some of these behaviors include:

- May avoid eye contact
- May prefer to be alone
- Difficulty in expressing needs; does not use gestures
- Insistence on sameness
- Inappropriate response to sound or other sensory input

- Difficulty interacting with others
- No real fear of dangers
- Apparent insensitivity to pain
- Avoidance of touch
- Sustained unusual repetitive play
- Uneven physical skills
- Uneven or missing verbal skills
- Inappropriate laughing or giggling
- Inappropriate attachment to objects
- Fascination with water, lights, and reflections
- Echoes words or phrases
- May seek sensory stimulation, including heavy pressure
- Spins objects or self.

Recognition

What a first-responding police officer may see and hear

Persons with autism will often look perfectly typical. Approximately 50 per cent of people with autism are nonverbal. They may not respond to a 'Stop!' command and may attempt to move or run away when approached. They may cover their ears or look away. They may not recognize a police uniform, badge, or vehicle or may not understand what is expected of them if they do. They may not be able to distinguish between a minor and a serious problem. They may appear as deaf. They may have motor-skill problems that will affect their gait. They may walk pigeon-toed, toe walk, and have difficulty running. They may be dressed oddly or without regard to the weather conditions.

Up to 40 per cent of the population with ASD may experience seizure activity by age 21 years. The seizure activity may not be apparent to the responder. The child or adult may have other medical disorders and may behave inappropriately because of non-autism medical conditions, such as asthma. A caregiver or service animal may accompany the child or adult. The person with autism may present an autism information card, wear medical alert jewelry, or have medical or identification information sewn or printed in permanent ink into inner or outer clothes or on nonpermanent tattoos.

Persons with autism do not react well to changes in their routine. Unexpected changes in routines, such as having suddenly to interact with law enforcement professionals or a sudden exposure to sensory stimuli, may cause the person's behaviors to escalate. Children and adults with autism may be sensitive to touch, sound, lights, odors, and animals. Light touch, such as a pat on the shoulder, can set off a behavior escalation. A heavy touch or deep pressure is often preferred to light touch. Seizure activity or behavior escalation can occur when there is exposure to loud noises, bright lights, strong odors, canine partners, or new, stressful situations. There may be similar reactions with exposure to certain foods. When their routines or atypical behaviors are interrupted, they may respond with aggressive behavior, such as screaming, hitting, biting, and kicking. They may injure themselves or others. They may not know how or where to get help. Persons with autism often have no choice in how they respond – the way they respond is part of their very nature.

Persons with autism may have difficulty in expressing their needs and may have difficulty using gestures. They may display unusual or repetitive physical movements such as rapid hand-flapping, finger-flicking, and twirling of hands or objects. They may spin their bodies or objects, rock back and forth, or pace excessively. They may become so fixated in these behaviors that they will not pay attention to anything else.

Those with autism may have difficulty judging personal space: they may intrude into others' personal space by standing too close, or they may stand too far away. They may have little awareness of private body parts. They may strongly insist on sameness in their environment. They may enter settings with a memorized preconceived visual standard, note any discrepancies, attempt to make adjustments to fit their standard, and violate the space and property boundaries of others. If blocked from reducing such discrepancies, tantrums may emerge that seem unexpected.

They will have difficulty interpreting body language, such as command presence or defensive posture, or facial expressions, such as raised eyebrows, rolling eyes, smiles, and frowns.

Those with verbal abilities may be recognized by their limited range of speech. They may display a limited vocabulary, or echolalia: echoing and repeating the words of others. Their speech may be monotone, computer-like, and with no inflection. If verbal, they may have problems using the correct volume for the situation. They may be observed talking to themselves or to no one in particular.

They may approach or talk to strangers. They may not be able to provide information or be able to answer questions. If able, the information may have no or little direct relationship to the matter at hand. They may have difficulty seeing a different point of view or being able to recognize a breakdown in communication. They often cannot integrate the perspective of others into their decision-making and make poor social judgments based on their inability to accurately predict the perspective of others.

They may not ask for clarification of questions or be able to fulfill a request for clarification of their responses. They may not be able to understand or accept a rational answer. They may not understand or respond to jokes, slang, innuendo, insults, or double meanings. Their behaviors may limit credibility with others. They are usually honest, do not lie, or are not very capable liars. They may provide blunt, often tactless answers. If you are too fat, they will tell you, as they will to stop smoking or that you are ugly.

Persons with autism may present as defiant, argumentative, stubborn, and belligerent, or as if they are under the influence of drugs or alcohol. They may be poor listeners, not seeming to care what is said to them. They may be unable to maintain eye contact even when others shift their position to obtain it. They may say 'No', 'Yes', or 'Why' to all questions. When uncomfortable or under stress, the verbal person may persevere on favorite topics as if trying to change the subject, ask repeated questions, engage in arguments or rambling speech, or lose the ability to speak (Hildebrandt 1993).

What are the common calls for assistance?

An understanding is beginning to emerge from the autism community of the predictability of the sometimes minor, sometimes severe incidents that result in calls for assistance to law enforcement agencies.

When in a place where they are unknown, persons with autism may display atypical behaviors that others view as suspicious. First-responders may encounter a person who is acting oddly on another's property, attempting to gain entry to a home, sitting in a lawn chair or swing, climbing trees, looking into the windows of homes, running into traffic, or dressed inappropriately for the weather or public view. Persons with autism may be unusually attracted to water sources and may be found splashing in fountains or attempting to enter pools or other water sources. This dangerous attraction has resulted in many drowning deaths.

Their need for sensory stimulation, motion, or touch may attract them to swings and slides. Adults of any age may be reported at playground swings and slides playing near children who are very significantly younger. Concern over adults engaged in this activity near children may lead to calls for a law enforcement response.

They may also be reported as an unknown person swinging on a stranger's porch glider. They may choose nonstandard swings, like a chandelier, light post, or basketball hoop. Others may be found stimulating their balance skills in dangerous places – for instance, river or lake break-walls, fences, cement walls, or bridgelike structures.

During their attempts at sensory stimulation, they may be reported running into walls, attempting to jump from a high place, or hiding under mattresses or heavy things found in a vacant yard or left out in the trash.

Whether in the community alone or with a support person, they may display behaviors, communications, and reactions to stimuli which others will find weird. Persons with autism have not developed the social awareness that is required in the community, and their actions, though not mean or malicious, can appear that way to others. Their behaviors may escalate quickly into tantrumlike behaviors, and they may not understand the consequences of their actions.

Persons with autism may have an obsession to make order of objects. On store shelves, items that are stacked backwards, upside down, or turned around may appear as out of order, and attempts to rearrange these items may be taken as shoplifting.

Persons with autism may follow or approach children, the elderly, or others that attract them, without an understanding of the social inappropriateness of their behavior. This may occur in stores, parks, airports, train and bus stations, and public restrooms and appear to others as stalking or as a prelude to assault or a sexual advance. Persons with autism may attempt to hug or touch strangers or may sniff all persons and objects that are new to their environment.

International border inspections, airport, building, and event security checkpoints, or anywhere that law enforcement professionals will examine others and expect appropriate answers to questions are places where persons with autism will likely have difficulties. Lights, sounds, objects, or the presence of canine partners at security checkpoints can cause a person with autism to react in inappropriate ways.

There may be calls to find a child or adult with autism who has apparently run away. He or she may be attracted to pools, lakes, or water sources. This topic is discussed thoroughly under 'Lost and Wandering' in this chapter, and under 'Elopement' in Chapter 8.

Response

What does this all mean for the first-responding law enforcement professional?

A caregiver will typically accompany children and adults with more severe autism. Adolescents and adults with less severe autism or with Asperger's Syndrome will have more independence skills and can be found in the community without a caregiver. Since every person with autism is different, some can have a combination of higher and lower ability skills. All groups will pose recognition and response difficulties for law enforcement professionals.

When responding to a call that involves a person with autism, officers may face a situation that will challenge the training, instincts, and professional conduct of even the most experienced police veteran (Debbaudt and Rothman 2001). Is the individual intoxicated? On narcotics? Or is the person developmentally disabled?

Escalated behavior

Perhaps the highest risk situation for a first-responding police officer is when the person with autism is demonstrating escalated behaviors.

Assistance or 911 calls could come from family members or caregivers who are seeking assistance and identify the person as having autism. A dispatcher may use a reference code – for instance, Code 20 in parts of Florida, a Code Mental in Detroit – that indicates to the first-responder that the call is a domestic situation involving a person with autism or other like condition. Such a call can cause extreme apprehension for first-responding police officers. These situations have the potential to result in violent physical confrontations between police and citizens.

While in transit to the scene, the first-responder will have a few moments to consider what may be occurring. It might just be someone with autism who is unknown in the area who is merely looking into the windows of a store while repeating a favorite phrase and flapping their hands. He or she might be having a seizure or reacting to the sensory stimuli – lights, smells, sounds – that are found in the neighborhood. The person may be covering his or her ears and shrieking, not knowing how or where to get help. It is possible that the person could have a form of mental illness or be having a psychotic episode, although the condition of autism itself is not a form of psychosis or mental illness.

Police may be called to intervene when the behavior of the child or adult with autism has apparently become escalated to a point beyond the control of care providers – for example, a struggle inside a vehicle or a parent restraining a tantruming child. While those in the autism community become accustomed to observing, understanding, and accepting most symptoms, behaviors, and characteristics of persons with autism as forms of communication, when observed by members of the general public the person with autism may be viewed as suspicious, threatening, or potentially dangerous.

While responding officers must always consider their own safety, as well as the safety of others, their presence may cause further inappropriate responses by a person with autism. Persons with autism may not know the implications of their behavior – they may not understand the consequences of their actions, especially aggressive actions. An officer's approach may cause people with this condition to flee, sometimes failing to obey an order to stop. Other people with autism may react by dropping to the floor or ground and rocking back and forth, averting eye contact with the officer. Officers should not interpret a person with autism's failure to respond to orders or questions as a lack of cooperation or as a reason for increased force. Although persons with autism are sometimes self-abusing, they may escalate into tantrumlike behavior (e.g. screaming, pushing, kicking, hitting) from fear, frustration, or confusion. They cannot conceptualize meanness or acts of purposeful injury to others. They just want the circumstances to change but do not know how to implement that change. This presents an obvious dilemma to responding officers (Debbaudt and Rothman 2001).

Seeking help from caregivers

After making the determination that another person at the scene is a parent, relative, friend, or adult careworker, the officer should seek information from that person about the circumstances of the incident, how to communicate with the person, and possible calming techniques to use. This person may possess knowledge or skills that allow an officer to successfully resolve the situation.

Officers must be alert to caregivers who are unable to respond to them. The following story illustrates this: On 30 April, 2000, Calvin Champion Jr., a 32-year-old Nashville, Tennessee, man, died after being pepper-sprayed, handcuffed, leg restrained, and forced to the ground by three police officers at a shopping center. After vomiting, his pulse became weak and he lost consciousness. He was pronounced dead after being transported to a nearby hospital.

When his paid personal-care attendant had first called 911 after the man's behavior escalated beyond her control, the call was dispatched as a domestic disturbance involving a man with mental retardation. The caregiver, who had only been on the job for two weeks and had decided to bring her three-year-old son along to work that day, failed to tell the officers that the man had autism until after they had subdued him. A 24-hour-a-day mental health Mobile Crisis Response Team, trained to apply crisis-management training in response to such occasions, was not called to the scene.

When a caregiver lacks the training or ability to provide critical information to the police and the responding officers have no training in techniques to de-escalate the behaviors of a person with autism, grave consequences can be the result.

De-escalation techniques

Persons with autism may have difficulty processing sensory information or adjusting to their sensory diet. They often have difficulties regulating their arousal levels due to their unique array of over- and under-sensitivities to routine objects and events. Their pursuit of or reaction to sensory inputs is largely determined by adjusting to the physiologic arousal.

The behavior of persons with autism may escalate in response to sensory stimuli – for instance, single or, especially, multiple flashing lights, shiny badges, sirens, loudspeakers or loud voices, perfumes, tobacco smoke, canine partners. They may become upset when their routine is changed. They may respond to stressful situations or an unexpected encounter with police with an escalation of self-stimulating behaviors that are not directed at another person, such as pacing about or hitting themselves. If there is no risk to the responder or to others on the scene, attempts should not be made to stop self-stimulating behaviors.

If verbal communication is unsuccessful, officers should look for the presence of medical ID jewelry, clothing tags, nonpermanent tattoos, or an autism information card. A person with autism, whether verbal or nonverbal, or an accompanying caregiver may present an ID or medical-emergency card. The person may have another medical disorder and behave inappropriately because of non-autism-induced symptoms, such as an asthmatic attack or a seizure.

The person should, if possible, be calmly guided to a quiet place and some space created. The officers should be a model of calming behavior: calm creates calm. The situation should be controlled using communication skills rather than physical skill. If possible, attempts should be made to remove or reduce any extraneous or even normal sensory input, such as multiple flashing lights or sirens. Law enforcers have suggested considering the tactics used in a hostage taking. In other words, time is on the officers' side; using it can make a big difference. The person should be shown that no harm is intended. To control the situation, the person should be guided to a place of geographic containment rather than being physically restrained. People with autism often need to move, pace, rock, finger-flick, flap, etc. to calm themselves. De-escalation should start to take place after a few minutes.

Custody: touching and physical restraint

In spite of every effort to avoid it, the first-responder may have to touch the person with autism – for instance, to prevent injury, to place the person in an ambulance, or to take him or her into custody. A person with autism may bolt and run if others are too close; on the other hand, the person with autism may her/himself get too close to others or rock in and out of someone's face. Light touch – a tap on the shoulder or light brush of the hair – can set off behavior-escalation or self-injury. Firm touch or deep pressure is a preferred approach for first responders. If individuals can be taken down quickly and receive pressure across their body and not just a hold down, they may respond well. Some individuals actually invite takedowns for this deep-pressure feedback. Many persons with autism are known to seek deep pressure, such as hiding between heavy mattresses or under heavy objects. Use of a buffer – a blanket, cushion, or vest – should be considered when attempting to touch the person. Officers should be alert to a person's sudden backward or forward lurches of their head.

Physical restraint should be used only after all other interventions have been tried and have failed. Restraint should never be the first reaction when a person with autism escalates. When first-responders, caregivers or teachers use physical restraint, not only do they risk injury to themselves or the person with autism, they also risk losing the trust of the person being restrained. Extreme care must be taken whenever restraining a person with autism. Never place a person with autism on his or her stomach. Persons with autism frequently have underdeveloped trunk, abdomen, and shoulder muscles or hypotonia. Placing them on their stomach may compromise their diaphragm, causing breathing difficulties. This action may lead to further struggle, often misinterpreted as attempts to get free, when actually the person is struggling to breathe. Many persons with autism also have seizure disorders or other common medical conditions such as asthma. Restraining a person during a seizure or asthmatic attack can cause injury or death.

Persons with autism should never have their arms crossed in front of them or be held from behind. This may, once again, compromise the diaphragm in those with hypotonia. A more effective method is to have people on both sides holding the upper arm and wrist areas. Once a person with autism is down on the floor he or she should be released and geographical containment should be used. Geographical containment is the preferred method of control for a person with autism: a safe space should be provided for the person to calm him/herself through movement, rocking, pacing, finger-flicking, hand-flapping, etc. Restraint may only serve to escalate apparently aggressive behaviors.

Emergency response
The first responder to the scene of a fire, accident, or other disaster may be told about or discover a person with autism. These types of situations will almost certainly cause confusion and stress for the person with

autism. The responder should work with caregivers who are present to safely remove the person from the scene. It is possible that the caregivers may themselves be the victims of the disaster, leaving the person with autism alone. The latter's reactions may become dangerous to him/herself and to emergency responders. It is necessary to be alert to attempts by that person to go back into a blazing home, or to pick up a sparking electric wire, or to flee into unsafe areas. If possible, information should be obtained about this person and his or her caregivers from witnesses, neighbors, or bystanders.

A person with autism should be carefully assessed for injury. This person may have an unusually high threshold for pain and be unable to ask for or seek help. If a determination is made that injury has occurred, the officer's response should consider the person's limited cognitive skills and atypical reactions to stress. It may become necessary to accompany this individual to a hospital or provide information and assistance to emergency medical responders. Remember that this person may be extremely sensitive to touch and other sensory input. Placing this person on a gurney and strapping her or him in should be done with extreme caution and sensitivity to her or his unique needs. Always alert emergency-room professionals about the person with autism and prioritize her or his emergency medical assistance, even if injuries or needs are minor. Waiting for treatment may trigger or escalate behaviors, contribute negatively to the person's medical condition, and increase the time and attention devoted to him or her by first-responders.

An autism response methodology

Understanding what autism is, and how to respond to those who have autism, is valuable information for law enforcers to use while performing their duties to protect the public, especially those who cannot protect themselves.

Since a call for assistance involving a child or adult with autism can occur anytime, anywhere, recognizing the symptoms of autism and knowing contact approaches becomes necessary for first-responders to avoid situations of risk. There are risks to the person with autism and responder, and there is also the risk of litigation if appropriate procedures are not followed.

Law enforcement officers are experienced and well trained in dealing with the unexpected encountered during situations to which they are dispatched. By understanding the nature of the disability of autism, responding officers can manage these situations more effectively. A useful methodology of dealing with a person who has autism can be outlined in a few short points using the acronym AUTISM (Debbaudt and Rothman 2001):

Approach the person in a quiet, non-threatening manner. Persons with autism may be hypersensitive to stimuli. Avoid quick motions and gestures that could be, even remotely, seen as threatening.

Understand that touching the person with autism may cause the protective 'fight or flight' reaction. Never touch the shoulders or near the face. Their hypersensitivity includes being touched and even extends to invasions of their personal space.

Talk to the person in a moderated and calm voice. You may have to repeat your directions or questions several times. Be patient and wait for answers that may be delayed. Raising your voice will not help and may be viewed as threatening.

Instructions should be simple and direct, avoiding slang. A person with autism will take what you say literally. 'Do you think that's cool?' 'What have you got up your sleeve?' 'Are you pulling my leg?' or 'Up against the wall!' are examples of phrases that probably will cause confusion and may cause an inappropriate response. Directions should be specific, such as 'Stand up' or 'Go to the car, now', and this will reduce the chance of confusion.

Seek all indicators to evaluate the situation as it is unfolding and be willing to adjust your actions accordingly. Visually evaluate for injuries because persons with autism can have an extremely high threshold for pain or be unable to ask for help.

Maintain a safe distance until any inappropriate behaviors lessen but remain alert to the possibility of outbursts or impulsive acts. Be able to retreat, if necessary, to de-escalate the situation until you can determine what is going on at the scene.

Offender trends, arrest, required legal warnings, and incarceration

Offender trends

To demonstrate to law enforcers the personal space and social-awareness problems that a person with autism frequently has, I tell a story at autism-awareness workshops about a typical summertime visit to the beach. To draw an analogy, I describe how anyone might observe someone walking on the beach in a skimpy bathing suit. Most folks would stand 40 to 50 feet away with sunglasses-protected eyes following the bather but the head remaining stationary. This is a socially appropriate way of checking out the curves and lines of the bather without making that person feel uncomfortable. For effect, I put on the sunglasses then take them off as my eyes follow horizontally as my face remains stationary and faced slightly away from the imaginary bather.

I quickly follow with an example of a young man with autism who might not bother with the social pretense. He would walk along with a female walking on the beach two feet away while checking her out without the aid of the sunglasses and without an understanding of the social inappropriateness. The bather may feel stalked and call law enforcement for help. As I tell this part of the story for effect I get too close to a member of the audience.

My son Kelly was in attendance at one of the law enforcement sessions two weeks before we took a summertime trip to one of Michigan's shoreline beaches. As we spread our blanket on the sand preparing for a day of swimming and relaxing, our then 16-year-old son noticed two older teenaged girls lying on their blanket perhaps a hundred feet away. Remembering my story from the police training session, he picked up my sunglasses from the blanket, walked to a distance of about ten feet from the girls, tilted his head strategically away from them, and stared away. He was halfway there in the social-appropriateness department.

My wife saw that the girls, having noticed Kelly a few feet away, were uncomfortable with his presence. She went over, explained autism to them, and introduced our young son. Once the girls understood that he meant no harm, their tension dissolved.

But what if my wife hadn't been there to explain? We could imagine a scene where law enforcers were called to respond, and my son freely and guilelessly admitting his transgression and being arrested for sexual harassment or stalking. He would only be doing what we all might do, but without the requisite social awareness. His actions would not have been understood by the victims or responding law enforcers. It would have looked like stalking or sexual harassment. For those who know the social tricks—in Kelly's case, sunglasses, extra personal space, tilt the head away—the actions would have been perfectly acceptable. For those that don't, trouble may follow.

There is no evidence to suggest that a person with autism is more likely to commit a crime than anyone else. Because a significant segment of this population will receive lifetime care or supervision, they may be very unlikely to commit a criminal act. But it can happen. To accurately and effectively file the initial report and ensure fairness, law enforcers will need to be aware of some common criminal situations that persons with autism may find themselves in, as well as of possible mitigating factors or aggravating conditions. Outlined below are offenses that have been reported in multiple cases involving persons with autism.

ILLEGAL ENTRY

Charges have been filed when the person with autism enters the homes or dwellings of others. In most of these cases, it is the lower-functioning individual who commits the offense, often during an elopement episode (see 'Lost and Wandering', this chapter). Depending on the level of understanding by the victim and prosecutor of the offense, someone who merely enters the home, disturbs nothing, and leaves may be referred for counseling and returned to the caregiver. But the caregiver's preventative actions may need to be scrutinized.

PHYSICAL STALKING, TELEPHONE AND INTERNET HARASSMENT

Persons with autism have difficulties in understanding social situations, customs, boundaries and norms. Understanding the feelings or point-of-view of others is frequently beyond their grasp. They may be unable to recognize the effect that their attempts at friendship will have on others.

For such a person, desperate to make a friend, the fact that his or her behavior may be unwelcome will be a difficult concept to understand. Even unsubtle clues, such as 'I'm married, go away, I'm not interested', may be misinterpreted by the person with autism as real interest. Facial expressions of disgust or anger that would ward off others may have no meaning whatever. He or she has decided to make a friend and may not take 'No' for an answer.

Persons with autism have the same desire to make friends as anyone but will run into difficulties when they seek to fulfill this desire. The social nuances of making friends will not be apparent to them. They may obsess and compulsively repeat actions that will be considered stalking by the victim and society.

Caregivers have reported cases where stalking has been charged against a person with autism who, looking for companionship, repeatedly shows up unannounced at the homes or workplaces of persons who later describe minimally knowing or having only met the offender briefly. The individual with autism may be under the impression that she or he has made a new friend, someone who wants to pursue a relationship, and will not recognize the verbal and nonverbal social signals of disinterest another person gives off. Similarly to stalking, someone else may feel intimidated by incessant phone calls or e-mail messages.

SEXUAL OFFENSES

When people with autism are charged with offenses that range from indecent exposure, public masturbation, or sexual harassment to more serious charges of criminal sexual conduct including rape, the person's sexual maturity and understanding of social norms should be questioned. While many persons with autism will have the same sexual desires as anyone, some may have no sexual desires at all. They may be touching others only because they lack awareness of private body parts. Those with sexual desires may not be able to experience or act them out in ways that are socially acceptable. They may sexually experiment at an advanced age, but with others significantly younger or older than they are. They may not know where the line is for mutual consent with a partner. Their crime may be less an issue of control than one of experimentation.

There may be the lack of understanding of their own or others' private body parts. They may not know how to hide their curiosity and will express it quite openly, perhaps in a public bathroom. They may not have learned where it is appropriate to gratify themselves, and where it is not. They may have learned to use these inappropriate public displays to get attention. In any case, others feel victimized and report the behavior to law enforcement agencies.

ACCOMPLICE OR CONSPIRATOR?

Cases have been reported where persons with autism have become involved in the criminal enterprises of others. Friendship and acceptance are typically the rewards offered for this involvement. In one case, an individual with Asperger's Syndrome who had excellent computer skills and access to sophisticated printing equipment was hoodwinked by others into producing counterfeit U.S. currency. In another case, a jewelry store worker with autism was manipulated by 'friends' into bringing samples from work. People with autism and other developmental disabilities have been reported by police as having been recruited by drug gangs as couriers or as foils in smuggling operations. Their reward was friendship and being able to hang out at the dope house. Persons with autism guilty of making bad friends may compound their mistakes by the actions they take in keeping them.

VIOLENT CRIME

There is an increase in cases where the person with autism has physically assaulted tormenters. Many of these reports of retaliation emanate from schools. Those with ASDs are often the targets of harassment, teasing, and bullying in the community and in schools. While assault can never be overlooked, the harassment of the individual can often be traced as the cause of the assault. There is more information on harassment and retaliation in Chapter 9.

Although rare, violent crimes have been committed by those on the spectrum. Cases exist where it is clear through the evidence that a person with autism has committed a crime of violence, such as rape and murder.

Any criminal act, especially a violent one, can become hard to understand and deal with. Such acts can occur without rhyme or reason. When these occur, the criminal justice system must always question intent, a necessary element of nearly every violent or other crime. In cases involving offenders with autism, it is a good practice to consider mitigating factors and aggravating conditions. Nevertheless, the person's autism must be recorded and documented in the initial report.

Arrest

There will be circumstances when a first-responder must take a person with autism into custody. For instance, police receive a call about a Peeping Tom. The first-responder arrives on the scene and finds a young man looking into a neighbor's window. The officer discovers from an ID card or from a relative who has arrived on the scene that the man has autism. Is this person looking into the window at a clock? At a clock on the wall in a room in which a woman is undressing? Or is he looking at the woman undressing? While the autism may be a mitigating factor, the first-responding police officer has an obligation to resolve the matter according to departmental policy and will take the man into custody.

At this point, the officer will file the initial report. For the case to be resolved fairly, detectives and prosecutors who will decide on a course of action must know about the person's autism. It is possible that the man *was* merely looking at the clock, an obsession associated with his autism. But without documentation in the initial report of the condition, a fair investigation may not be possible. In any case in which a person is found to have autism and is taken into custody, it is critical for the first-responder to follow procedure and document that he or she has learned that the person has autism.

Required legal statements

Many people with autism will not understand the concept of constitutional rights. Their use of language is usually concrete and literal. They may understand a request to waive their right to remain silent as a question about whether or not they can wave their right hand or arm, than answer yes and waive their rights. It should not be assumed that such persons truly understand a Miranda warning or any other legal statements that officers are required to recite.

Incarceration

If an individual is taken into custody for whatever reason, and the officer remotely suspects or comes to know that the person has autism or another developmental disability, the officer should err on the side of caution and safety and request that jail authorities segregate the individual. The individual should never be placed in the general incarcerated population before being evaluated by a mental health professional. They would be at extreme risk in that environment for abuse, injury, or both. A caregiver or community health professional should be contacted immediately.

Once the determination has been made that the individual has autism or is developmentally disabled, this must be included in the report. Documenting the offenders' autism in the initial report will ensure fairness, accuracy, and the best possible conditions for any follow-up investigation.

Lost and wandering

Providing care and security for those with autism presents difficult challenges for families and caregivers. Parents report elopement as a major concern for many of their children. When children or adults are prone to elopement, the challenges will test the mettle of the best parents and caregivers. The runner escapes, swiftly and unexpectedly, when caregivers are otherwise occupied, even briefly. But despite the best prevention efforts, elopement still occurs.

The terms 'elopement' and 'runners' describe situations and children and adults with autism who are prone to escaping into the community from homes, from schools, or while shopping or traveling. Adults can wander away from group homes and caregivers, but the majority of lost and wandering calls will involve children; the reporters will be their parents.

The elopement problem is enhanced since runners typically do not conceptualize that they are running away. They may just be returning to a favorite place or going back to look at something attractive, recently seen through the car window on a trip. *They* are not lost, and they are very content to be where they are. However, to the general public, unattended children are a cause for concern which is usually followed by a call to local police (Debbaudt and Rothman 2001).

Since many with autism have no recognition of real dangers, the results of elopement are too often tragic. Law enforcement professionals should be especially aware of the proclivity of children and adults with autism to seek out water sources regardless of their inability to swim. Multiple occurrences of drowning deaths have resulted from episodes of autistic elopement. Parents and caregivers become frustrated in their attempts to prevent elopement and fearful of what will happen when they cannot. The problems created by elopement for parents and caregivers are discussed further in Chapter 8.

First response to elopement

First-responders may be familiar with the issue of elopement from experience with elderly citizens with Alzheimer's disease who may also wander in the community unable to provide their name, address, or phone number and who may become aggressive when approached. In the case of autism, frantic parents, annoyed neighbors, or concerned citizens often call the police and the police typically respond, not only by finding the child and returning her or him home, but also by treating the youngster to a ride to the station, complete with flashing lights and whooping sirens. In an effort to make the lost child feel comfortable, police often give tours, treats, and lots of attention (Debbaudt 1994).

Yet, such well-meaning responses are not right for a child with autism. The 'found' child may not respond well to the officer's efforts at consolation. Children and many adults with autism usually cannot process multiple stimuli at one time. Flashing lights, whooping sirens, canine partners, perfume, after-shave, or tobacco smoke may overload fragile sensory systems; certain foods may interfere with strict dietary concerns. The resultant behavior patterns may make it impossible for the officer to return the child and may jeopardize the safety of those involved in the incident. Conversely, the treats and attention of the police may lead to repeated occurrences since the child is, in effect, being rewarded for the behavior (Debbaudt and Rothman 2001).

Skepticism

Many runners become excellent escape artists. They seem to have an uncanny sense of when to run and how to undo locks and turn off alarms. A parent taking a phone call or giving attention to a sibling acts as a cue for the runner to take off. Runners often outlast sleepless, exhausted parents and escape into the night. When elopement involves children, law enforcement professionals may become skeptical about the circumstances of elopement, view parents as neglectful or incompetent, and make referrals to social service or child welfare agencies. Parents who find themselves under scrutiny by the criminal justice system have temporarily lost custody of their children, accused of parental neglect. To retrieve their bewildered children from temporary foster care, parents will plead their cases to judges and prosecutors who have little understanding of autism. Parents who appear in court to disprove neglect allegations can pay a heavy legal and emotional toll. While merely being the parents of a child with autism serves as no guarantee that they are *not* negligent, even responsible prevention efforts can be misconstrued as parental neglect.

Skepticism by responding officers is understandable. After all, who wouldn't question the parents of a child who repeatedly escapes the family home to run through a neighborhood at all hours of the day and night? What would an officer think when they return a child to a home where all the interior doors were padlocked and all the windows barred? Without knowledge to the contrary, this could appear as evidence of parental neglect or abuse. Law enforcement responders will need to rule out parental neglect, but in cases of autistic elopement occurrences of this are rare.

Personal location technology

Communications technology is now being used to track the movements of Alzheimer's patients and others who bolt and wander. Radio and global positioning system (GPS) technologies utilize transmitters worn by the individual that emit signals that are transmitted to antennae and satellite receivers. The signal allows responders to hone in on the location of the lost or missing person.

When necessary, these technologies can provide for quicker and more accurate and effective ground, air, and water-borne responses by search and rescue teams. When compared to often cumbersome and expensive searches involving foot patrols, tracking animals, vehicles, and aircraft, communications-based tracking systems are potentially useful. But both technologies are dependent on caregivers and on the willingness of law enforcement agencies to make the financial commitment. With usage and production increases, communications technologies should become more advanced and less costly for the consumer.

ID jewelry

First-responders can look for medical alert bracelets, lockets, shoe tags and clothes labels, and washable tattoos. Although some runners will have sensory issues that cause them to remove unfamiliar items – such as high-tech transmitters or labels sewn into their clothes – from their bodies, emergency ID jewelry or tags are an option for some. For those who will wear them, these items can help responders become aware of their identity and possible medical needs.

Home security

Referrals to information about basic home-security techniques can be offered to parents and caregivers. There is a wide selection of low- to high-tech options to consider for doors and windows – for example, dead-bolt locks, alarms, and motion and sound detectors. Law enforcers can develop a basic brochure or survey for those unfamiliar with home-security techniques. Families can be urged to consult a professional locksmith and private-sector home-security consultant.

First response awareness programs

Elopement, misidentification, safety, and security of their vulnerable loved ones with autism are serious and growing issues for parents, caregivers, educators, and adult home operators. Families and caregivers are trying their best to help resolve a problem that they are usually just becoming familiar with, and they will depend on local law enforcement agencies for help in this area. Awareness, swift reaction, and sensitivity will become necessary when addressing these concerns.

Critical information handouts for 911 systems

First-responders consistently identify having personal information about an individual available to them at the time of dispatch – such as a description of the person's unusual behaviors and where they might occur, de-escalation techniques, and a person's likes, dislikes, or fears – as their best chance to provide better recognition and response to the person with autism. Parents and caregivers are starting to understand the need for developing and distributing handouts proactively to the police and other first-responding agencies. The following is a comprehensive handout checklist that has been developed specifically for this purpose (a completed sample handout can be found in Chapter 8):

Person-Specific Handout Checklist for 911 Systems, First-Responders, and Emergency-Room Staff

Name of child or adult

Current physical description of
child or adult, including height,
weight, eye and hair color, any
scars or other identifying
marks

[Recent Photograph]

Name of parents or care
providers

Address

Phone numbers – home and emergency, work, cell, pager

Emergency contact-person information

Sensory, medical, or dietary issues, if any

Inclination for elopement and atypical behaviors or characteristics that may attract attention

Favorite attractions and locations where person may be found

Favorite toys, objects, or discussion topics

Likes, dislikes, and approach and de-escalation techniques

Method of communication, if non-verbal – sign language, picture board, written word

ID wear – jewelry, tags, on clothes, nonpermanent tattoo

Map and address guide to nearby properties with water sources and with dangerous locations highlighted

Blueprint or drawing of home, with bedrooms of autistic individuals highlighted.

A model program

Local law enforcement agencies in the United States have developed response programs to address chronic elopement. The Eugene, Oregon Police Department provides a model. Their Community Policing Support Team has developed the *Special Needs Awareness Program* (SNAP) to identify and safely return to their homes people with Alzheimer's and autism, and others who may wander and are unable to communicate and/or remember their names or home address. The program is completely voluntary.

When a person joins SNAP, their computer generated photo will be added to the program with their consent, or the consent of a parent/guardian. This can be accomplished by either scanning a recent photo or by bringing the individual to the Police Department to have their photograph taken.

The SNAP program will: contain a picture of the individual along with their family's, or care provider's information; conduct a search by physical description to identify the individuals who can't identify themselves.

Only law enforcement agencies in Lane County will have access to the database and *only for the purpose of identifying SNAP participants*. (Eugene Oregon Police Department 2000)

Law enforcement agencies that work with parents and caregivers in local communities to develop, increase, and expand information in their emergency systems – for example, the *Special Needs Awareness Program* – will give their officers better first-response information. Parents and caregivers who let neighbors, local law enforcement, fire, ambulance, and emergency-room professionals proactively know that they are responsible, knowledgeable, and approachable about children and adults with autism can effectively increase the odds for a better response and understanding when incidents do occur. While there may be no panacea for dealing with these issues, families and caregivers who address them with the support of their local law enforcement community will find the best results in these prevention efforts.

Law enforcement agencies can suggest that families input the emergency response 911 systems with this information. Consider contacting the local Autism Society or the school district to circulate the availability of this service. It may be in the best interest of all concerned to have the families return the checklists as one to ensure the ease of entry into the 911 systems.

Law enforcement organizations that make themselves available as a resource – for example, by making referrals to an Alzheimer's group for support or by speaking about home safety or the 911 emergency systems at an Autism Society meeting – demonstrate not only compassion, interest and concern to families and caregivers who are facing the difficult issue of elopement, they demonstrate their commitment to public safety in the communities they serve.

3

Interview and Interrogation
of Persons with Autism

Conducting on-scene interviews of victims, witnesses, and suspects, a routine event for patrol officers, allows the officer to gather basic information such as who, what, where, when, and why. The officer uses this information to assess situations and decide on further action.

An interrogation differs somewhat from basic fact-gathering since it tends to focus more on a subject who probably is suspected of a criminal act. Different techniques, rules, and procedures apply during an interrogation. A law enforcement professional may be trained in the techniques of interrogation, the rules that apply – such as when to advise suspects of their legal rights – and what procedures to use – such as the venue, environment, or comfort level of the suspect. An interrogation is conducted when there is reason to suspect that a person knows more about or was involved in committing a criminal act.

Whether it is a simple field interview or a more focused interrogation, dealing with persons with autism presents unique challenges and considerations.

Misleading indications of guilt

There will be occasions when first-responders refer a case involving a person with autism to the detective bureau. In most cases this will involve an individual who apparently communicates well and has achieved a high level of independence in the community. The person may have been found at or been identified by others as being at the scene or possessing knowledge of a crime.

Higher-functioning or more independent individuals with autism may live alone or without constant supervision, be able to drive or use public transportation, hold a job, and enjoy leisure activities. They may possess apparently normal verbal skills but be deficient in comprehension, social awareness, and decision-making. They may appear as quite normal at first, but the symptoms, behaviors, and characteristics – for example, providing blunt or tactless answers, changing the subject, or being unable to understand or accept a rational answer – will become apparent to the educated investigator. However, without an understanding of the disability it will be easy to misinterpret the information provided as an indicator of guilt.

They may provide no eye contact at all, even when a questioner shifts their position to obtain it. The person may have been taught to give eye contact but this may be perceived as insincere, glaring, or fixated. The interviewer may mistake this unusual eye contact as a tension-relieving technique used by a guilty person, when it is nothing more than a symptom of the condition of autism.

When stressed, communications skills may diminish or disappear. Answers may seem evasive or unconnected to the question that was asked. Individuals may appear belligerent, argumentative, stubborn, or inattentive – behavior that may seem indicative of a person with something to hide. They can easily become the object of increased scrutiny by the questioner. What started as a routine fact-gathering task may turn into an unnecessary interrogation because an officer, unfamiliar with the behaviors of ASDs may have had their law enforcement instincts rightfully aroused.

Possible traps when interrogating a person with autism

Techniques used during interrogations may include the use of trickery and deceit. 'Without some elements of "trickery", such as leading the suspect to believe that the police have some tangible or specific evidence of guilt, many interrogations will be totally ineffective' (Inbau and Reid 1967, p.196). 'Only one important qualification has been attached to the rule; the trickery or deceit must not be of such nature as to induce a false confession' (Inbau and Reid 1967, p.195).

The higher-functioning person through his or her responses, and the unaware interrogator through their beliefs, may become unwitting accomplices to continuing a faulty investigation in the best case or, in the worst case, to extracting a false confession.

The following are some possible traps that interrogators can fall into when conducting the interrogation of a person with autism.

MEMORY SKILLS

Interrogators should understand that the person with autism may have highly developed memory skills. The person may have learned to commit facts or the statements of others to memory. This rote skill may allow him or her to quickly assimilate and regurgitate data. The individual may be more proficient in his or her expression of these facts than in comprehension of them. He or she may have developed a sophisticated form of echolalia, echoing and repeating the words of others. For example, the person with autism could memorize the allegations of a citizen overheard at the scene, facts inadvertently provided by a first-responding officer, and details of some of the circumstantial evidence that an interrogator has revealed during questioning. Under these circumstances, the person with autism could provide a very convincing untrue statement or false confession. At the least, this knowledge could be misconstrued as real familiarity of facts that only a guilty person could know.

THE INTERROGATOR AS AUTHORITY FIGURE

Persons with autism may have been conditioned through their lifetime to look to authority figures to make many of life's important decisions for them. They have learned to depend on and trust these authority figures to be right. The interrogator may be viewed as another authority figure that is always right. 'If he thinks I robbed the bank, maybe he's right' is a conclusion that the confused person with autism may develop during an interrogation.

FRIENDLY–UNFRIENDLY

Persons with autism may have a hard time developing friends. They may seek the friendship of others, only to be continually disappointed. They may repeat social gaffes that others find repelling, and they may learn little from these friend-seeking experiences. Although they may not have learned how to make a friend, this will not stop them from trying.

The interrogation techniques of friendly–unfriendly interrogators have the potential to produce false confession from such persons. 'The friendly–unfriendly act is particularly appropriate in the interrogation of a subject who is politely apathetic – the person who just nods his head as though in agreement with the interrogator, but says nothing in response except possibly a denial of guilt' (Inbau and Reid 1967, p.64). The person with autism may involuntarily give an interrogator the impression that he or she is apathetic, and may deny guilt because he or she is innocent.

The friendly interrogator may convince the trusting individual that they are, truly, their friend. The person with autism has now just made a new friend, and 'if my friend wants to know about me robbing a bank, then I'll tell him just to keep him around.' Rather than telling the truth, the person will tell his or her 'friend' what he or she thinks they want to hear.

CONCRETE THINKERS

Persons with autism are concrete thinkers. Jokes, sarcasm, innuendo, satire, trickery and deceit are difficult concepts for them to understand and appreciate. Their world is unadorned with pretext, pretense, sham, and dishonesty. They are naturally guileless and very honest. They are not very able liars. They expect others to be honest and they can become confused or disappointed when they are not. When an interrogator makes a promise, such as 'When you tell me about robbing the bank, I promise to keep it a secret', the person with autism may believe the promise to be true. We have learned that persons with autism may not have a complete understanding of what is expected of them, or the consequences of their actions. They may not understand how serious the consequences of the confession will be for them. They may be led to believe that lying is what is expected of them.

POOR LIARS

An interrogator may seek an admission of lying about any part of the alleged offense. The person with autism may try to respond to this new friend or authority figure with what he or she believes is the reply that is wanted. The person may truly have made a mistake; to the interrogator, it was a lie.

When asked if he or she has ever thought about committing the offense in question, the honest-to-a-fault but innocent person with autism may answer 'Yes', as opposed to the characteristic answer of 'No' from an innocent person. While both persons only thought in passing about committing such an offense, the 'normal' person would not consider answering yes. The concrete-thinking autistic person may answer the question as asked, causing the interrogator to continue the probe.

It is possible that the person with autism has learned through experience to lie. But her or his attempts to lie will be done poorly. An interrogator should ask a series of unrelated questions to determine the person's ability and potential for lying. This should be done prior to asking questions that are pertinent to the matter at hand.

Tips for the interviewer/interrogator

The interviewer must be specific in what information is sought by asking questions that avoid ambiguity. If the interviewer asks, 'Did you take the money?', the person with autism may say 'Yes' whether or not she or he actually took it. It would be clearer to ask, 'What did you do?' allowing for the individual to provide a response. If you ask, 'Were you with your family or John?' the autistic person may respond, 'John', because that was the last choice of the sequence. If the question was asked again but in reverse order, the autistic person may answer, 'My family,' for the same reason (Perske 1991). A more specific question might be, 'Who were you with?' which reduces the influence of suggestion on the subject. Obtaining a false confession is a situation for which no conscientious law enforcement officer would want to be responsible.

Some other points investigators may consider:

- Be sure the subject understands his or her legal rights. Saying yes is not the same as understanding them. To the concrete thinker 'waiving your right' may mean waving your right hand.

- To avoid confusion, ask questions that rely on narrative responses.

- Asking a yes or no question is an essential and important element of determining guilt. But consider asking a series of yes or no questions to determine the style and dependability of the response. Then ask the key yes or no questions.

- Seek the advice of a psychiatrist or psychologist who is familiar with autism. Consider contacting a specialist in autism from outside the criminal justice system.

- Seek the advice of a prosecutor. You have a job to do and want to perform it in the best way possible. With their unusual responses to your questions, the higher-functioning person with autism may challenge all of your training. Follow procedure, but also follow your gut instincts if you feel that something isn't 'quite right' with the subject of your investigation. Like the old adage, if the statement or confession is too good to be true, it probably is.

4

Victims with Autism

Persons with autism, parents, caregivers, and advocates often find it difficult to talk about stories of victimization and abuse. These incidents are living hell for persons with autism and the worst nightmares for parents, advocates, and those who care. Lack of credibility as a witness or reporter of facts will often leave the person with autism in the unenviable position of being victimized twice: once by the abuser and again by a system that lacks the ability or resolve to understand him or her. For those who are victimized, there can be lifelong traumatic effects. Law enforcement professionals can assist to obviate this problem through becoming aware of the settings of victimization and abuse and by developing effective ways to combat it. Law enforcers can take accurate and usable statements during interview, and thereby improve the credibility of and positive outcomes for the victim/witness who has autism.

Perfect victims

An analogy can be made between victims with autism and tourists traveling in a foreign land. Their style of dress and awkward sense of native customs makes both stand out in a crowd. They may stray into unsafe neighborhoods, unaware of the risks. Criminals with ill intent, adept at selecting their next victim, will pick them out of a crowd, follow them to a perfect location away from any scrutiny, and commit their crimes.

When tourists seek help from local authorities, they will have difficulty describing the incident with clarity. The foreign-language phrase book is of little use. They struggle to use words picked from a traveler's dictionary, which do not convey the traveler's meaning. Double-entendres, colloquialisms, slang will be beyond their reach. Their body language and gestures will not be understood, could be taken out of context, or may be mistaken as being obscene or threatening. Without a personal interpreter, they will not be able to communicate. Their lack of ability to express themselves will clearly frustrate any hope of finding justice. The police officer will dutifully take a tourist's statement knowing that it will be of little use in prosecuting the offenders. Whereas the tourist may accept his or her fate having at least received the benefit of a lesson about safety and security, the person with autism won't even gain that much. Lacking abstract-thinking skills, persons with autism will not conclude that their dress, speech, and isolation were the keys to their victimization; thus, they will not change and they are likely to be victimized again.

Persons with autism are not only perfect victims, distinguished by their enigmatic demeanor and inability to express themselves convincingly, but these characteristics may also cause them to become permanent captives of injustice when they travel this often bleak, never-ending road. While *they* may know and understand perfectly well that they were victimized, those who lack the training to distill their intent and meaning will not understand their communications. Even when the victim with autism can relate the incident, prosecutors may be reluctant to present them to judges and juries who may find the victim's physical presence and communication style – the very symptoms of autism – to be less than convincing.

Identifying situations of abuse

Victimization may come from likely sources, such as criminally bent individuals looking for easy prey and purveyors of hate and ignorance, but it can also be perpetrated by those known to the victim such as paid caregivers, members of the immediate family, neighbors, coworkers, students, and other persons. Abuse can occur wherever a person with autism lives, is educated, spends leisure time, or works.

Neighborhood resentment

It is no secret that group homes for persons with developmental disabilities have long been subjects of fear and targets for resentment in the community. Under the federal Fair Housing Act, it is illegal in the United States to alert neighbors when a person or group of persons with disabilities moves into a neighborhood. Neighbors are often left with the erroneous impression that the area property values will plummet. Equally erroneous are mythical beliefs that persons with developmental disabilities are dangerous and inconvenient burdens on society. Neighbors will find it hard not to be influenced by this faulty mind-set, their discomfort from the daily physical reminder that disability could happen to them, and their awkwardness when they are around their new neighbors with disabilities. Their ignorance kindles a fear of the unknown.

Neighborhood fear and resentment can be attractive, fertile breeding grounds for organized hate groups. Organized hate groups and other misguided individuals have been known to target residents of group homes for abuse, intimidation, and violent acts. Any area in which a group home is located should be monitored closely for the presence of hate graffiti, flyers, posters, club houses, or negative public sentiment.

Criminal gangs

Criminal-gang activity should also be monitored relative to persons with autism. Gang members are known to recruit those with disabilities as runners for drug and other criminal activities. Gangs can also offer a form of belonging or friendship that an isolated person with autism may be drawn to. The person with autism may only want to make a friend and may therefore not recognize that her or his vulnerability has been targeted or that she or he is being abused and manipulated by criminal-gang members.

Physical intimidation

Persons with autism can often be the target of bullies, teasers, and tormenters at school, at workplaces, and in their neighborhoods. They may not be able to speak out or defend themselves or even be cognizant of the fact that they are targets of this activity. The abusers will continue without a second thought about being caught or punished. Bullying, teasing, torment, and harassment often escalate when perpetrators do not fear discovery. Harassment can lead to physical assault. Investigators should conduct interviews in schools, neighborhoods, and workplaces to locate witnesses or other victims of disability harassment, assault, or intimidation.

Adult care facilities

Adult care facilities, group homes, and assisted-living situations are attractive to an abuser. The work force in this industry is underpaid and often undertrained. Persons who are abusers are reportedly aware that employment in this industry will give them easy access to victims who are unable to report abuse, or whose reports will not be taken seriously by management or law enforcement.

Theft

Thefts of residents' money and belongings are also commonly reported at adult care facilities. A resident of an adult care facility who has autism may be vulnerable to petty thefts by staff, visitors, or other residents. Corrupt caregivers, telemarketers, and visitors have targeted residents with a variety of scams, cons, and get-rich-quick schemes, especially at times when government or insurance aid checks are disbursed.

Sexual abuse

Because of their sexual naiveté and often passive nature, the person with autism can become the perfect prey for sexual abusers. Women are especially vulnerable to sexual assault. A person with autism may have heterosexual or homosexual interests or be asexual, having no interest at all in sexual relations. Another form of abuse is encouraging those with disabilities to abuse each other. For their apparent self-amusement, workers have encouraged residents to assault each other sexually and physically. Investigators will need to consider a possible lack of awareness by the victim of what a sexual assault is. Sexual abuse can occur at any living facility, whether or not the victim is completely or partially independent or receives full-time care.

Eye contact

Because of the importance that people with normal social skills place on appropriate eye contact, there is a tendency in the educational community to encourage those with autism to develop the ability to make eye contact with others. Unfortunately, however, the development of this skill in those with autism has a downside. Often when the person learns to make eye contact, she or he then has a problem in knowing when such eye contact is inappropriate. There are situations in everyday life where gaining and maintaining eye contact is not a good idea, as, for example, when one is on a crowded urban subway or street. Especially troublesome for some individuals with autism is making eye contact in a public restroom. It certainly is not a good idea to seek and maintain eye contact in the men's room of an interstate-highway rest stop. Yet some individuals with autism have not mastered this delicate concept of human communication. Combined with a lack of awareness or naiveté about appropriate sexual behavior, the person with autism may be unwittingly giving signals that she or he wants a sexual encounter. The person in these situations can become victimized easily or be accused as a perpetrator.

Investigating allegations of abuse

Officers investigating complaints involving victims with autism must consider that while this may be the first report of physical assault, harassment, abuse, etc., such incidents may have occurred many times in the past. Crimes against persons with disabilities too often go unreported and are certainly underreported within the adult care industry, schools, and workplaces.

There are some options for law enforcement professionals when considering abuse or victim reports by persons with autism. First of all, caregivers and law enforcers should always take seriously disclosures from people with autism about abuse or victimization. Great care must be taken to guard against other, perhaps well-intentioned, persons poisoning the well of information by interviewing or getting into too much detail with the person with autism before investigators can conduct an interview. When parents, advocates, school administrators, or others hear an abuse report, their first response should be to call the police.

There will be cases where it will be self-evident through injuries that abuse has occurred. In other cases, there will be allegations without or with little physical evidence. In the latter situations, to ensure fairness, investigators should be careful to conduct good victim/witness interviews to determine whether false allegations are present. In any case, interviews should be conducted with all potential witnesses away from the site of the allegations and without the scrutiny of those who may have a vested interest in the outcome, such as school or group-home administrators. Witnesses who are employees may feel intimidated by having work superiors either present during interviews or aware of the fact that they are being interviewed about the allegations.

Investigators will need to review the training and background of any individual in abuse cases. Interviews may need to be conducted with residents of care facilities to determine whether abuse, even if unintentional, is widespread. The backgrounds of those involved in these cases should be thoroughly checked for other abuse allegations, as should their work and relocation histories.

Frequent change of employment, and/or frequent relocation, by someone employed in the adult care industry should be investigated for the reasons why it has occurred. It is not uncommon for abusers to be fired or transferred when allegations of abuse are reported to institutions but not to the police. This practice – found, for instance, in religious institutions until recently (Schaeffer 1998) – allows perpetrators to continue their abuse elsewhere. Administrators may also be sensitive to their own faulty pre-hiring investigations or due diligence, to negative publicity, and to loss of contracts with public health agencies. Administrators often make the poor assumption that the abuse cannot be proven and the allegations are never reported to police.

Interviewing the victim/witness

During the investigation phase, law enforcers can better interview witnesses with autism by seeking assistance from professionals and/or advocates in the disabilities community. Through this cooperative effort, investigators can overcome the communication difficulties that these cases present; at the same time they become more familiar with autism, thus increasing their own skills in dealing with members of the disabilities community. Such outside professionals can be as useful as having an interpreter present when interviewing a witness who does not speak the native language. Of course, professionals who do assist must realize that they, too, could be called as witnesses in any ensuing court proceedings.

Walter Coles developed an interest in issues facing people with disabilities while serving as an officer with the Royal Canadian Mounted Police in 1988. He subsequently worked on a collaborative effort that resulted in the curriculum, 'Admissible in Court: Interviewing Witnesses Who Live with Disabilities' (Hutchinson MacLean 1998). The following are tips for interviewers including points suggested by Walter Coles and curriculum collaborator, writer and occupational therapist Pip Farrar, adapted from her book *End the Silence: Preventing the Sexual Assault of Women with Communication Disabilities: Developing a Community Response* (1996).

Preparation:

- Discuss with the prosecutor any plan of action.
- Interview the caregiver or person who took the report first.
- Investigate possibility of multiple victims – interview others with whom the perpetrator had contact.

- Review any records of assessment that the person or their caregiver can provide.

- Ensure that assessment records are fresh, not outdated.

- Seek out from records the person's communication strengths – the goal is to prove competency of witness.

- Interview caregivers and persons who 'know' the victim for tips about how the person gives and receives information.

- Investigators should get to know the person and their style of communication through casual conversation *before* they attempt to get any recollection from them. If they are not verbal, how do they communicate?

Videotaping:

- Consider videotaping the interview. (A good video interview with a victim who a perpetrator believes could not provide information may be a key to inducing the perpetrator to confess or plead guilty.)

- Discuss with the prosecutor an intention to conduct two videotaped interviews.

- If not considered prejudicial, proceed with preliminary videotaped interview to become acquainted with witness.

- Do not discuss the alleged offense during the first interview. Save direct questions about the offense for the second interview. However, if the witness makes a spontaneous disclosure of abuse, then proceed with details.

The interview:

- Carefully plan questioning based on the person's ability level.

- Formulate and write down questions that are developed around the person's communication abilities.

- Consider having a trusted caregiver or autism professional at interview.

- Avoid all extraneous sensory distractions; the person may be easily distracted.

- Avoid uniforms or 'authority' clothing.

- Develop good rapport; use the person's first name.

- Do not be condescending. If the victim is an adult, do not treat him or her as a child.

- Be careful to avoid witness burnout.

- Use simple, direct language. Deal with one issue at a time.

- Get the witness to recreate context of the event in his or her own words.

- Make sure your words and their words have meanings that you both understand.

- Be alert to nonverbal cues – for example, restlessness, frowning, or long pauses between answers – that suggest the witness does not understand, is confused, or does not agree with the question you asked or the statement you made.

- Make sure that you and the witness understand who is being referred to when using pronouns.

- Keep length of question short; avoid questions that suggest multiple answers.

- Be patient; wait for an answer.

- The witness or victim with autism may not want to answer any question more than once.

- Ask victim first if it is OK to repeat a question.

- Let them know it is OK to say 'no' to your questions.

- Be convinced that the victim understands or is known to tell the truth.

- Carefully establish time lines. Rather than asking about the specific time of the day or dates, broader questions focusing on context may be more useful. For example, finding out if the witness has a fairly routine schedule may provide cues about day and time.

- Avoid leading questions.

- Consider conducting the interview in short time spans; the person may have a short attention span.

What law enforcers can do for victims

When abuse is reported and investigated, law enforcement and criminal justice professionals may be constrained from prosecuting by rules that are tilted against the victim and towards the accused. While there may be evidence of a crime, the victim's credibility often becomes an issue for those who prosecute it. The victim who may not be able to report the facts in a credible way will find justice difficult to obtain. When crimes are reported, there is often a lack of credibility for witnesses with autism. As a result, many crimes may not be reported at all.

Law enforcers can investigate abuse against persons with autism and other developmental disabilities more effectively when they take the time to become better educated about the condition, the individual, and the settings of abuse. This process, although time-consuming, can also become a valuable learning tool for any investigator. Assigning an experienced investigator with others who have little or no experience is recommended since it allows for the experience to be passed along if a senior investigator retires or is transferred (Hutchinson MacLean 1998). While it may be difficult for law enforcers to investigate, the person with autism has the same rights as anyone to justice when allegations of abuse occur. Positive resolutions to these cases can be obtained when investigators are well prepared for success.

5

Law Enforcement
Training Programs

To get a sense of what life is like for the person with autism, officers should be encouraged to visit schools, workplaces, homes, and Autism Society meetings, where they can see what people with autism look and sound like. Officers can develop an eye and ear for autism. These visits can enhance officers' observation and communication skills and give persons with autism a close-up look at police officers in a relaxed atmosphere. These interactions can take away some of the mystery of autism to officers and make officers seem more approachable to those with autism.

Operation Mainstream, for example, which resulted from the Guido Rodriguez Jr. incident described in the Introduction, is a decidedly proactive, informal approach to improving the interactions between law enforcers and those with autism and other developmental disabilities. The program offers training to youngsters with disabilities to help make their encounters with police more positive. In addition, it provides police officers with the opportunity to observe first-hand what is the normal behavior of those with autism.

Randomly picked officers spend an hour a month with students with disabilities. The students gather around the officers, who sit among them rather than at the teacher's desk, and ask questions. The students learn things about the officers – like the fact that they may be dads and moms – which make them seem to be more than just police officers, or strangers. The officers conduct mock interviews with students in which they pretend they have just met students on the street. They ask the students what their names are, where they live, what their phone numbers are, and if they have identification cards. Students may also get a tour of the police car. Parents and caregivers are given details of the program and are encouraged to discuss the experience with their children. The response from parents, teachers, caregivers, students, and law enforcers has been overwhelmingly positive.

Autism does not have to be invisible. Training tools – for example, the Maryland Police and Correctional Training Commissions curriculum *Why Law Enforcement Needs To Recognize Autism* (MPCTC 1999), and the *Autism Awareness Video for Law Enforcement/Community Service Personnel* produced by Judy Swift (1998) for the Harrisburg, Pennsylvania, chapter of the Autism Society of America – have been developed to help educate law enforcers, especially first-responders, to see and hear autism in the individuals with whom they may have contact. The tools also address elopement, de-escalation, custody, interview/interrogation, and victim issues, situations that are increasingly common and predictable for law enforcers when they encounter individuals with autism. Law enforcement agencies across the United States are now embracing these tools to train their workforces. The fact that these tools even exist indicates a need for autism education for law enforcers.

Training, school resource, youth section, child abuse, and community liaison officers may find autism training especially useful. Police supervisors, investigators, interview/interrogation specialists, customs and immigration, building and retail security, department of corrections professionals, defense attorneys, prosecutors, judges, psychiatric forensic experts, social service and child welfare agency employees, and legislators also have a stake in learning about the issues involving individuals with autism.

6

Conclusion

With over twelve million persons affected worldwide, including a new, alarmingly higher-incidence generation that is rapidly maturing, basic law enforcement recognition-and-response techniques are needed to guard against unintentionally focusing law enforcement resources on individuals with autism simply because autism was not properly identified. Responding to predictable law enforcement and criminal justice situations involving children and adults with autism will become increasingly more common and will require better training for law enforcers.

The implications for law enforcement agencies that do not recognize the need for training are obvious: lawsuits, negative public scrutiny, a loss of credibility and public confidence for the department and its officers by citizens in the communities they serve. In hindsight, it becomes easy to criticize the actions of law enforcement professionals. Officers should not be expected to do a field diagnosis for autism, but, without some type of training, good officers are left to their own experiences to deal with the complexities of autism. Typically, the officers' training in these areas is either nonexistent or outdated.

Legislation has been passed in some states that requires disability training for law enforcement officers. Support by autism advocates for mandatory law enforcement disability-training legislation should not be construed as anything other than their desire to guard against the loss of good programs due to changes in administrations, transfers, or retirements and to guarantee the best training and practices possible for law enforcers.

With a wider awareness of the issues, the global law enforcement community should anticipate the approaches of autism advocates who want to develop mutually cooperative, information sharing partnerships. In the best spirit and practice of community policing, programs that develop real education and understanding should be welcomed and encouraged by law enforcement agencies, parents, and caregivers. After all, we have the same goal in mind: safer communities.

SECTION TWO

The Citizen's Perspective

7

Introduction

There's really no way to prepare yourself for hearing from a stranger that your child has autism. For my wife, Gay, and me, the stranger who told us that our son, Kelly, had autism was an esteemed psychiatrist at Children's Hospital of Michigan in Detroit. We were driving home on that sunny spring day in 1987 as I thought about the first time I had heard the word autism. It was in the early 1970's while I was watching a nationally televised fundraiser that was organized and hosted by a Hollywood actor, the late Lloyd Nolan. I recalled the aging actor's desperate plea for funding and understanding for his son and others who had autism. The lasting image of autism I came away with that day was of a young, nonverbal boy who wore a hockey helmet to protect himself from self-inflicted head banging. With the psychiatrist's words echoing in my mind, I remembered the image of that boy. That isn't Kelly, I thought.

As we drove home, we recalled when we first began to feel concern about Kelly. After his second birthday, we observed Kelly playing around but not with the other kids in the neighborhood; we decided to get him some structured contact with his peers. We enrolled Kelly in nursery school a month before his third birthday. His speech came late and seemed repetitive, yet he could sing every word of the American and Canadian national anthems in perfect pitch. We started private speech and language therapy. When he had trouble drawing and holding a crayon, we brought him to a physical therapist for sessions. When we called his name it seemed as if he didn't hear us, although he would tell us he could hear our friends' car minutes before it turned down our street. We discussed the doctor's advice during our drive home. We were becoming aware that there was something very different about our beautiful, tow-headed child.

We brought Kelly to Children's Hospital to get a specialist's opinion. After several sessions that included videotaped play, games, tests, and interactions with the staff, we were given an appointment to come to the office without Kelly. In a nice manner, but with little fanfare, the doctor said: 'Your son has autism. There's no cure. He'll always seem odd or different to others but with special help he can learn some independence skills and, hopefully, to read and write. He'll have difficulty accepting changes in his routine. He has a fascination with letters and numbers and will take great comfort in these things since they will never change. There's no way to determine what life will be like for him as an adult, but you, as parents, can make a big difference in how he learns and accepts autism.'

We wanted to know if we had done something to cause autism. Was it in our genes? A birth trauma? Were we bad parents? The doctor told us that they didn't know what caused autism. It was something that some kids were born with. The doctor suggested we find out all we could about autism and get involved with a support group. He recommended that we continue with any programs the school system offered.

We both grieved and cried during that drive home. But we also came to the conclusion that our attitude toward our young son and his disability could make a big difference for him. It was, after all, his life we were talking about, not ours. And we vowed in the car that day to do all we could to educate ourselves and our son about autism. We would find a way to give him every opportunity to live a full, independent life. Autism or not, we would show the world to Kelly and show Kelly to the world.

That decision has become our guiding light to finding the best that life has to offer for Kelly. But our story is not remarkable in the world of autism. Parents everywhere have similar stories to tell. Hundreds of times every day, another family learns that they have a child with autism.

Like us, many of these families get much strength and support from the autism community, whose members consist of parents and all persons affected by autism. We'll try anything to help our kids. We freely share our success and failure stories with each other at meetings and conferences, in newsletters and books, and on the Internet. When something doesn't work, we try something else. We find doctors, educators, specialists, programs and techniques, good and bad, and tell each other about them. We encourage professionals to learn more about our children. We get better at letting them know what works as they become better at finding new answers.

But, ultimately, it's our kids who teach us the most about autism. They possess the amazing ability and perseverance to get through the awesome roadblocks that autism often places in front of them. Our son is just one of the many millions with autism who go beyond any dreams we might have had for them. I'm embarrassed to admit the many times my son has made me look like a Doubting Thomas. But I doubt him no more. Kelly has taught me more about autism than I could have ever imagined.

The learning process can get ugly, though. We spend money we haven't yet earned on therapies, diets, specialists, books, and videos. Private insurance or school district funds rarely cover this. Vacations? They became an excuse to run up the credit-card bill to attend a conference several states away or spend weeks at a time in a foreign country to get that certain therapy that would help our son. There are no vacations from autism. Time off work? Who cares, when it might make a positive difference for our son. It's taken a financial toll on our family over the years. We've learned that many families in the autism community have fallen into this same trap. But it's hard to put a dollar figure on doing the right thing for your child.

In our family, we share caregiving in ways that best reflect our skills. That means that from early on, Gay, whose manual and artistic skills are strong, handled the basics like dirty diapers, feeding, shopping, and laundry. As Kelly grew, so did her participation, from being a teacher's aide to planning and participating in craft projects for Kelly's classes to volunteering for class trips. Now that Kelly is older, she teaches and supervises his grass-cutting and snow-blowing jobs and is his primary on-the-road driving instructor. My caregiving has been to take Kelly for trips to the park and to ride the bus to Tiger Stadium for baseball games, to read him books, or just to play with him. Swimming is a physical activity he enjoys and something we've done together regularly since he was a small child. I've served in various capacities with our local autism societies, including being involved in public-awareness campaigns. I've been blessed with having a supportive partner who bears the brunt of the day-to-day challenges, allowing me the time to participate as an advocate in the autism community. This active participation keeps us well informed on autism, which is critical to us for making sound decisions about Kelly.

But even when you take the time to learn all you can and apply what you learn, there are other problems areas in dealing with autism. There is, for example, the isolation that many of our families encounter. We learned early that in order to go to a support meeting, workshop, conference, or even have a night out with friends, you often do it without your partner. Baby-sitters who agree to come more than once are as precious to parents as diamonds or gold. But it's more likely that one spouse or the other cares for the kids while the other attends a meeting. There can be a lack of understanding by friends, neighbors, coworkers, even within families, about how daunting apparently simple everyday errands can become. Shopping, dining, and housekeeping – tasks taken in stride by others – can become high stress, anxiety-ridden adventures. The lack of understanding serves to separate us from the outside world. It's as if we've been entered into a contest without ever having filled out the entry forms. It's difficult to put into words the feelings you have. Sometimes you just want to scream out for help. But, more often than not, these feelings never leave the privacy of your home or your mind.

Another tough lesson I learned early on is how some people react to our loved ones who have autism. One learns quickly about 'The Look'. This is the face of ignorance and disgust, perhaps even fear, that we try to ignore when we are in public places: the sneers, frowns, upturned eyebrows, backward glances; the hurtful, whispered comments – Get that child under control! What kind of parent are you? What are you doing to that child? Why don't you give the spoiled brat a good whack? Get him out of here! – heard while shopping, at a movie theater, or even in church. These looks and comments can burn deep into the hearts of parents who are doing their best to control an upset child.

You cope by trying to see their side. (They don't understand that this child is using every ounce of his ability just to go into a crowded store. They aren't aware that parents have no choice but to take their child with them. They have no idea how hard it is to find childcare for a child with a disability. They probably can't even tell he has a disability. They probably aren't aware that community experiences are recommended for children and adults with autism. They probably don't even know what autism is. Then how would they know how disturbed someone with autism may be from the sensory input of a store's lighting, unusual sounds or odors, even the presence of strangers?) You remind yourself that autism is visible only to those who live with it or are trained to see it. But the reactions, the looks, still hurt. Often they discourage families from trying to get out into the community even once in a while. The lack of awareness and understanding can be devastating, even perilous.

There have been so many times during our lives with Kelly that this lack of understanding has caused problems. I recall a day in 1988 when I took him to a nearby shopping mall as I had done many times before to give my wife a break. It was also a chance for the two of us to get some exercise and spend some time together.

After parking our car, we entered the mall near a strategically located toy store. I believe that it is an unwritten international law that every mall must have at least one toy store located at its entrance. Needless to say, we found ourselves in that toy store. We agreed that Kelly could get a car from the toy store. But we disagreed as to what kind. Kelly wanted the two-hundred-dollar, battery-operated drivable model. My choice? The eighty-nine-cent Hot Wheels miniature. Since I was paying, I felt it was my choice to make. When my son become upset over my choice, his behavior escalated into lying on his back on the store's floor, kicking and shrieking. Having decided it was time to leave,

I picked up my red-faced and teary-eyed son, put him over my shoulder, and carried him from the store to our car in the mall's parking lot. I noticed The Looks we were getting from others as we left, though by now I was used to them.

No sooner had I strapped Kelly into his car seat than I saw that our car had been blocked from leaving by a mall police car. A young officer got out of the patrol car, walked over to our car, and peered in at my son. I listened and watched from a few yards away as the officer pointed at me and asked my son several times, 'Who is that?' Kelly's only response was more shrieking and crying.

When I finally asked the officer what the problem was, he told me he was responding to a report of a possible child abduction from the mall. I produced my driver's license and explained to him that Kelly was my son and that he had autism. I told him that my son became upset in the toy store and that I picked him up and carried him out. Although I didn't know it at the time, this became my first autism-awareness session for a law enforcement audience. I did a lousy job. Seeing the disbelief on the officer's face, and already feeling pent-up anger and frustration with the Lookgivers, I gruffly told the officer that he had two choices. He could arrest me and take in my screaming son as well, or he could back his car up and let me leave. I'm not sure if it was Kelly or I who convinced him, but he went back to his car, got in, and backed it out of our way. In my rearview mirror I could see him writing down my license-plate number as I drove away.

That was the day that I first thought about what life would be like for Kelly when I was no longer there to act as his interpreter and ambassador to the world. We had come to expect attention whenever we shopped, dined, or traveled with our son, but this experience with the police was something new. It made me focus on our mortality and ask what it would be like for him as an adult during the thirty-five or more years when he would no longer have us there to explain his autism to others or explain others to him. That experience in the mall left me more acutely aware of the need for better public awareness of autism. I began to realize that I had to do more than just feel angry and frustrated about what others didn't know about autism, especially when the others were key members of the community, like law enforcement professionals.

Autism awareness materials for law enforcers did not exist at that time. Drawing on my experience in private-sector law enforcement and freelance journalism, I began a search for information to change this. In 1991, a national call to the autism community for information and personal experiences between those with autism and law enforcement professionals was published in the Autism Society of America's *Advocate* newsletter. It netted over 150 responses. They included personal stories and news reports from people with autism, parents, advocates, and educators. The research continued for eighteen more months and consisted of interviews with law enforcement and autism professionals; reviews of related curricula and published reports; contact with authors, researchers, and advocates; and a steady two-way stream of information, letters, and phone calls to parents and persons with autism. The culmination of this was my booklet, *Avoiding Unfortunate Situations: A Collection of Experiences, Tips and Information from and about People with Autism and Other Developmental Disabilities and Their Encounters with Law Enforcement Agencies* (1994).

The booklet's publication received a great deal of interest and feedback in the autism community. Professionals in the field told me that this was an area that had been overlooked; some said that law enforcement issues had been kept in the closet so as not to further stigmatize those with autism. Most importantly, it opened the doors for further discussion of the issues involved with autism awareness for law enforcers.

A lot of valuable advice, support, and encouragement for my work has come from self-advocates, parents, and professionals. I've been honored to speak to autism audiences at conferences and workshops. I've been fortunate to collaborate on awareness projects with professionals in law enforcement and autism, including film-production and curriculum writing experiences. It's been my privilege to continue to report about these issues in autism publications and at conferences over the years. I've been given the opportunity to conduct in-service training sessions and workshops for law enforcers. The concern, advice, and information that others freely share has expanded the base of knowledge that is now available on this subject.

This book is an attempt to make that knowledge available to the law enforcement and autism communities and to all others with an interest in this area. It may help stimulate someone to write an article or make a film, or an autism advocacy organization to make autism/law enforcement issues a permanent agenda item, or encourage a researcher to track these issues. Perhaps a parent or caregiver will share some of the prevention tips, or an educator will be moved to make such training a staple of law enforcement education. If its content helps one police department avoid a lawsuit, if it helps a single police officer, defense lawyer, prosecutor, judge, correctional officer, or forensic expert ensure justice for a person with autism, or if it helps even one person with autism successfully navigate an encounter with law enforcement, it will have been worth the effort.

This section of the book is especially for the autism community, including those with autism, their parents, caregivers, and advocates. It is based on the shared experiences of hundreds of families who hope that what they have learned can help others in this close community live a little more easily within their larger communities.

8

Safety at Home
and in the Community

All parents want to provide their kids with safety and security. Parents
of kids with autism are no different. But the challenges we face are often
very different from other families. This Chapter provides some insight
into two important areas of risk for our loved ones: the problems of
elopement and misidentification. It also offers suggestions for prevention and for dealing with the situations when they do occur.

Elopement

The term 'elopement' refers to the repeated behavior of fleeing or
running away from home that is engaged in by some children and
adults. The person who practices this behavior is often referred to as a
'runner'. In this section, we take a look at elopement and discuss ways to
address it.

It is a cause for concern when a wandering child is observed alone in
the community. Depending on the behaviors they may exhibit, adult
runners, too, may be a cause for concern. A call to the local police typically follows. Sometimes the police pick the runner up and return him
or her safely home. In other cases, police can become suspicious about
the circumstances of the incident and call in social service or child
welfare agencies for further investigation.

Too many elopement incidents have ended in tragedy. It is all too common to hear about the first-time or chronic runner who finds her or his way to a pool or water source and drowns. Adults have wandered away from family or group homes, never to be heard of again. Others wander onto busy highways or through any unlocked door, oblivious to such risks as fast-moving traffic, dangerous animals, or angry neighbors. Regrettably, you won't know you have a runner until she or he runs. And by then it may be too late. The best advice for parents and caregivers of those with autism is to prepare for elopement whether or not that person is a runner.

Home security

A survey of the home to determine vulnerability is necessary. Doors and windows are the obvious escape routes. Since elopement protection is often designed to keep people *in* a dwelling, fire and disaster safety protection must also be considered. Extra alerts for fire, carbon monoxide, and disaster must always be considered as a key element of elopement protection.

A floor plan of the home should be prepared which includes particular bedrooms and locations where, in emergency situations, the person with autism may be found. Exterior window decals for emergency responders can be considered for bedrooms. The Autism Society of Illinois is a source for autism-specific decals. Floor plans that include the bedrooms of the autistic child or adult and any atypical behaviors the person may display during an emergency should be made available to fire, medical, and other emergency response agencies that serve the local community.

Securing the home is typically the first line of defense for elopement prevention. Double dead-bolt locks that require a key to get in or out are commonly used but should only be considered in conjunction with an emergency release system. Always consult with a home-security consultant or professional locksmith before installing double dead-bolt locks or any elopement-protection device. Window locks, door alarms, and sound and motion detectors can also prove to be useful. Perimeter fences and outdoor motion detectors provide a second line for many families. Home-improvement and security companies and professional locksmiths may provide free consultations for those interested in elopement-prevention ideas.

Emergency identification

Some type of ID wear is essential for those with autism, especially if they are nonverbal or are unable to respond to questions about their identity if they are found. Bracelets, anklets, necklaces, shoe or jacket tags, ID cards, clothing labels, or permanent ink ID on T-shirts or undergarments are all good options. The problem is that the person with autism who has sensory issues and finds IDs uncomfortable may remove them. An innovative option is the use of prepared, washable tattoos that bear ID information. If ID wear is used, first-responders may not know what autism is. More specific language should be considered in addition to name, address, and phone number, such as: nonverbal; sensitive to light, sound, or touch; possible seizure activity; or may not seek help.

Personal tracking technology

Some who elope are also adept at circumventing prevention measures and at picking the perfect times to do so. Parents preoccupied with other children or caregivers with other clients afford perfect opportunities to elope. Being briefly distracted on the phone is another. Exhausted parents report nighttime elopement, especially through windows, as a common problem. Any device that can quickly alert a caregiver to elopement can be a potential lifesaver.

Communications technology offers some hope for chronic elopement. Radio frequency (RF) tracking devices are in use in the United States by individual families and law enforcement agencies to track persons with Alzheimer's disease, Down's syndrome, mental retardation, and ASDs who have chronic wandering issues. Tracking devices that utilize GPS technology are also appearing in the marketplace. Both technologies require the users to wear a wristband transmitter that allows responders to locate the runner via RF or GPS. A person wearing the device who leaves a preset perimeter would trigger an automatic alert to caregivers. For RF devices, the caregiver would be alerted through a special beeper; with the GPS system a beeper or direct phone call from the monitoring service may be used.

For GPS users, the call center would immediately begin to track the movement via GPS signals to a computer-generated mapping system, call 911 or a prearranged emergency number, and supply the real-time location to parents, caregivers, or emergency responders. Radio-frequency devices require the caregiver to call emergency responders who must have matching locating equipment. The search needs to be conducted immediately, and emergency response teams must be familiar with and trained in its use.

The upside for RF technology is its dependability when the systems are in use. A problem with the GPS technology is coverage through buildings and over certain terrain. An upside with GPS, however, is that multiple perimeters can be set and easily changed with the call center, allowing coverage while traveling or in other locations such as schools. Maintenance must also be considered. With both technologies monthly maintenance involves changing wristbands and batteries. The problem with tracking devices, and ID wear, is that sensitive wearers may remove them.

As these products become more widely used, competition and new research will bring rapid improvements and cost reductions for consumers. Information about price, availability, demonstrations, and group presentations can be obtained from the manufacturers.

Community Awareness
PROS AND CONS

From a safety standpoint, caregivers accompanying those with autism should always have handout sheets with them, preferably with a current photograph. Handouts should also be used to prepare airport, customs, and immigration security personnel when traveling and should be given to security personnel and other key persons, such as local shop owners or managers, at locations frequently visited. These community-awareness measures may save precious time, even a life, should a person with autism elope.

But for some, safety is not the only issue; they consider such community awareness to be a privacy issue. One expert, Susan Moreno, in her publication *High Functioning Individuals With Autism* (1991), acknowledges two schools of thought on privacy: 'Some parents and teachers feel that the odds for safety are enhanced by providing basic information to key people... Others feel that sharing information is seldom or never necessary.' According to Moreno, those who don't believe in providing information may think that it leads to prejudgment of an individual, or that it is an invasion of, or a failure to respect, personal dignity. This decision by family members is also influenced by how the person with autism functions in the community.

While Moreno believes that there is no clearly right or wrong decision on this subject, her own experience leads her to believe that it is helpful if community members, especially public safety personnel, understand the potential problems of the developmentally disabled population.

DANGER ZONES

Parents and caregivers should develop an emergency list that includes the location of all water sources, train tracks, high traffic and accident areas, blind spots, stores, shopping centers, parks, playgrounds, golf courses, or any other nearby areas that may be dangerous or of interest to the runner. These areas should be searched first when elopement occurs. The names, addresses, and phone numbers of the owners of these properties should also be included on this list so that quick contact can be made. Some designation of neighbors who are more apt to be home, like retired persons or stay-at-home parents and workers, is also a good idea so they may be called first. Water sources, including children's and full-sized pools, ponds, streams, lakes, and larger bodies of water, are especially attractive to those with autism.

EYES AND EARS IN THE NEIGHBORHOOD

Quick response to elopement is the most critical element in avoiding a tragic outcome. In those first critical moments, informed neighbors are a most valuable asset. Those additional sets of eyes and ears may prevent a tragedy. At the least, they may prevent an unnecessary encounter with law enforcement. Most neighbors will appreciate knowing about those in their neighborhood and tend to look out for those who are more vulnerable. When one establishes good rapport with neighbors, it is much easier to identify where dangers or attractions to a runner may be. Neighbors, for example, know who has a swimming pool, or a mean dog, or which neighbors may be helpful in an emergency, such as the off-duty fireman or the mother who is also a nurse. They can also help identify those neighbors who may be unapproachable or are troublemakers.

INFORMATION FOR NEIGHBORS

It should be decided in advance what information to present to neighbors and other community members. A brief visit, introducing them to the family member and giving them a simple handout containing the name, address, and phone number, may be a good way to avoid problems down the road. It also gives a feel for what kind of person the neighbor may be. It might be felt appropriate to explain that the child or other family member may wander off from time to time and that a call would be appreciated if the person were seen alone in the neighborhood. Any questions that may be asked should be answered, but it may not be necessary to give out further information.

KNOW THE NEIGHBORS

The local police should be contacted about crime statistics in the neighborhood. While they may not identify a particular person or address, statistics about neighborhood crime trends can be obtained. Some caregivers may be apprehensive in talking to strangers about their kids who run, but it's often the devil you don't know who poses the most risk. If there are doubts about a neighbor, an investigative firm can be hired to obtain public-record documents about certain addresses or persons.

Alternatively, the agency can conduct a simple awareness campaign or survey and report about any suspicious responses. If there are other families in the area who are also concerned about elopement, private agencies may offer a lower price to conduct such an investigation.

EXTRA PRECAUTIONS

The issue of child abduction will need to be considered by parents of any child. For those kids with autism who elope, precautions must be taken. Keeping current photographs or video and fingerprints of the child is essential. Parents can purchase fingerprint kits, use them, and keep the prints at home. A note should be made of what the child is wearing each day. While it is true that family members, not strangers, are involved in the vast majority of child-abduction cases (Lord, Boudreaux, and Lanning 2001), elopement increases the minimal but frightening odds. There are open missing-persons cases throughout the world where the child or adult with autism has disappeared after elopement episodes. In one sad case, the eloping child was found murdered after being raped.

Some families who care for persons with chronic elopement issues, with other safety issues such as suddenly running out into the street, or with behavior issues that make the person stand out in the neighborhood have been successful in having traffic-warning signs erected with the words 'Slow: Person with Autism in Area'. In the United States, these signs are recognizable by their diamond shape, yellow background, and bold black graphics and printing. Even when a driver does not know what autism is, the sign itself is an indication to slow down and be on the alert. These signs can also be useful tools for starting general public awareness of autism in the community. Families in Michigan and Louisiana have successfully lobbied local law enforcement or government agencies for permission to have the signs made and erected.

Awareness campaigns are always an individual choice, but they are recommended as an effective tool to combat elopement. Taking these precautions may seem like overkill to some, but parents, law enforcement officers and adult care professionals have indicated the wisdom of them.

What causes elopement?

Those who have no history of wandering off may first do so when the family is at home. Or they may bolt away from parents or caregivers while out shopping, at a park or event, or on vacation. It could be that they are curious and just exploring, returning to a place of interest they have seen while riding in a car or on a walk with parents or caregivers. Some are apparently obsessive-compulsive or impulsively attracted to certain people, objects, locations, or structures. Curious and unable to tell anyone about it, they set off in search of something or someone they have found attractive on a recent car trip. Strangely, there are multiple reports of children and adults who are attracted to clocks and who wander peering into homes in search of them and entering homes where clocks are seen. Others are reportedly attracted to water spigots and will go from home to home turning them on. Some apparently run from sensory input; others to sensory pleasures. Runners may not feel that they are lost and will fail to seek help from others; they just keep going.

ANALYZE THE BEHAVIOR

Some cases of elopement will cease when changes in the home environment or the person's behavior can be made. A functional behavioral analysis can be performed to determine some of the reasons for elopement and may offer some solutions. One expert on behavioral plans is Margaret Creedon, Ph.D., an ASA Panel of Professional Advisors member and founding member of the Task Force for Prevention of Abuse to Persons with Developmental Disabilities. At the 1996 ASA National Conference in Milwaukee, Wisconsin during a session titled 'Strategies For Safer Interaction Within Communities' Dr. Creedon recommended a functional behavior analysis for those who elope.

Dr. Creedon reported that persons with autism might find even a familiar situation or a neighborhood activity too demanding because of sensory and/or information changes and may then 'run'. Sometimes they may need to reach a particular person, object, space, or activity and so 'run'. Once this occurs, strategies in addition to vigilance can be employed. Appropriate strategies for avoidance of overload stress use the person's communication system and provide for opportunities to 'take a break,' initiate a relaxation or self-calming technique acceptable in different environments, and have an alternative place or activity pre-arranged. If an individual is a collector of items – for example light bulbs – or is fascinated with such things out in the community as a hose running water, additional learning programs are needed. At the same time, a behavioral plan to monitor or limit the amount and time of access to certain persons or things can be implemented. Appropriate choices, denying or delaying access to an object, must include options for what else can be collected (Creedon, Debbaudt, and Campbell 1996).

Parents and carergivers may want to enlist the help of an autism specialist to conduct the analysis and develop a plan of action. An analysis may uncover sensory distractions in the home that the person is seeking to escape from, including smoke, pets, sounds, and lighting. Recollections of negative experiences – for instance, incidents with dogs or certain people or places – can trigger elopement events. There may be allergic reactions occurring even to normal carpeting, paints, or furniture.

Attractions for the person may be the architecture of homes or neighborhood landmarks – church steeples, for instance. Homes and parks may have fascinating features like swings, slides, and fountains. The attraction may be other children, adults, or pets. Once again, water sources are known to be attractive and potentially deadly lures. Also appealing and dangerous are cars, trucks, trains, and buses. Close attention should be paid to busy streets, traffic patterns, parking lots, and train tracks. Notes should be taken and a log kept on the patterns of elopement in order to predict occurrences and discover favorite places where the person may be found.

Dr. Creedon suggests the use of video and photographic examples as aids, with rule-repetition and role-rehearsal as training options.

Learning how to negotiate a space will depend on the individual's particular perceptual motor abilities and comprehension of the rules of everyday physics. One can learn to 'look both ways' and yet stop in the middle of the street to look at a moving vehicle. Rules that can be rehearsed in different formats must be generated. Task analyses must take the point of view of the person with autism (Creedon, Debbaudt and Campbell 1996).

One mom in New Zealand discovered that her son was attracted to vacuum cleaners and would escape at any time in search for them. After putting up flyers at appliance repair shops and flea markets about her son's fascination, her garage became filled with used Hoovers. Now happy at home with his newfound gadgets, his case of elopement was solved.

Parents and caregivers can develop a plan based on an analysis of environmental factors that cause the person to bolt or elope. The plan should be specific to the child or adult with autism, designed to avoid, anticipate, and respond to an occurrence of elopement, and shared with anyone who cares for that person, including teachers, classroom aides, relatives, friends, baby-sitters, and respite care staff.

Misidentification in the community

Parents and caregivers will also need to prepare for the possibility of others who may misidentify outbursts as abuse or assault to the person with autism or to the caregiver. The act of providing comfort or care to someone during an escalation of behavior can be misunderstood, such as the misidentified child-abduction incident I described with my son Kelly at the mall. Parents and caregivers have reported struggles with kids of all ages that resulted in first-responding law enforcers using force to intervene – the sad Calvin Champion Jr. death, for instance (Chapter 2). Our loved ones' innocent but obsessive touching of adults, children, pets, or items in stores may be seen by others as a crime in progress. Educational campaigns for law enforcement professionals are always useful, but caregivers will need to anticipate and prepare for the misidentification and reporting of their own actions and of the person with autism's behavior, as a crime.

Awareness for store security

A teenager or adult with autism who touches or makes order of items and products in stores may be mistaken for a shoplifter. Others may impulsively pick up a favorite item and run from the store without any intent of stealing. It will become necessary to identify the retail outlets and malls that families and caregivers frequent and to alert storeowners and employees to this person's activities before they happen. Security personnel should be prepared by giving them handouts including photographs prior to traveling or at locations that are visited frequently. Having a handout ready that at least includes a picture, description, specific instructions for appropriate responses and de-escalation techniques, any allergies or medical issues, phone numbers, and personal identification including address and emergency phone numbers can make a crucial difference to store security if they must search for or interact with a person with autism.

Adult care workers should receive regular training on how to interact with law enforcement professionals. Caregivers of persons who need assistance may find ID cards useful if approached by store security or police officer. Security professionals and police officers report that they would respond better to a person or caregiver who presented them with an ID card or handout that contained autism information. The more information a first-responder has available, the better chance she or he will have for a successful resolution to the call for help.

ID wear is essential and should be considered whenever a caregiver is in the community with a person who cannot communicate or is unable to present identification. Whenever traveling or in other community settings, such as shopping malls, amusement parks, or zoos, parents and caregivers should always be prepared with a handout sheet or business card to give to onlookers. A business-card handout for community members might contain a message such as 'Perhaps my son/daughter's behavior is surprising to you. This is because he/she has autism', a brief definition of autism, and the phone number/website address of a local or national advocacy organization.

Identify and change behaviors

Young children should be helped to understand the social rules of the community. The rules will need to be explained in detail. They need to know early on that touching items is only done when they are going to buy the item. Nothing should ever be put in their pocket. They will need to know that people need space and that touching someone they do not know is inappropriate. The older child can be observed at a discreet distance as he or she interacts with others in the community, with the carer alert to any problems that may arise and ready to intervene. But a note should also be made as to what behaviors are attracting others and this information used to coach the child on ways to improve. Repetition, role-playing, and monitored independent community experiences can be very helpful lessons (Debbaudt 2000a).

Emergency response systems – 911

Requests to have critical information entered into police or emergency response 911 systems are reasonable and are recommended by law enforcement. Individuals can refer their local law enforcement agency to the Eugene, Oregon Police Department *Special Needs Awareness Program*, information about which is described here in Chapter 2. Law enforcers have suggested that parents and advocates should provide them with potentially life-saving information about the possible behaviors that a person may display during an emergency, such as fleeing back into a burning home, picking up a sparking wire, running into traffic, behaviors that may be misidentified as suspicious to others, any medical issues, the presence of ID jewelry and tags, personal-location technology, and basic autism recognition and response techniques. The model SNAP program is voluntary for families. The information remains confidential and is protected from release to any other agency.

Law enforcement and emergency response professionals strongly suggest that parents and caregivers should visit nearby police stations, fire houses, emergency medical services (EMS), and hospital emergency rooms and should brief staff about the person with autism. Proactively providing information to key community agencies, such as police, fire, ambulance, and emergency room is highly recommended to prevent misidentifications and misunderstandings. Distributing a handout with full information is the best single action that parents and caregivers can take to allow for a better, informed first response.

Beyond law enforcement and fire agencies, emergency medical technicians (EMT), and local emergency rooms, this information should be circulated to trusted neighbors and multiple copies kept handy for whenever shopping, traveling, or in the community with a person with autism.

A good handout would include all the information necessary for a responder to know about the person with autism if the caregiver were to become incapacitated or unable to communicate. The Person-Specific Handout Checklist presented described in Chapter 2 outlines the information that a handout should ideally contain. A completed sample handout might look like this:

Michael Bradley

Male, seven years old, three feet, ten inches, 75 pounds, blonde hair, blue eyes, one-inch scar at hairline on left forehead, slight gap between upper front teeth.

[Recent photograph]

Parents are Susan (mother) and John (father) Bradley.

1234 Maple Street.

Phone numbers: home (313) 555–1111; Father's work (248) 555–2222; Pager (313) 555–3333; Mother's cell phone (313) 555–4444.

Emergency contact person: Kathy Avery (aunt) (248) 555–6666; Rita Jones (neighbor) 1256 Maple Street (313) 555–7777.

Michael cannot swim. He has asthma; at times he needs an inhaler to breathe. He is allergic to penicillin and dairy products.

Michael may be attracted to the church steeple and bell at St. Mark's church located at 788 Elm north of the Franklin senior citizens' complex. He will follow garbage trucks and ice-cream trucks whenever he sees or hears them in the neighborhood. He loves water and could be found at the fishpond near 1122 Maple or at the above-ground swimming pool in the backyard of 1088 Maple.

Michael is fascinated with circles and will search for any item with a circular shape, such as car taillights, balls, rings, can lids, coins. These items can lure him into potentially dangerous situations, a coin or bottle cap in the street, for instance. Any circular item could also be used to gain his attention and compliance.

Michael also likes Matchbox miniature toy cars and will comply with simple requests when one is offered to him to play with. Michael will typically follow simple instructions from anyone who talks about fire engines or Winnie the Pooh characters or when an apple is offered as a reward.

Michael is afraid of dogs and balloons and would run into oncoming traffic if in the presence of or faced with either.

Michael will flap his hands rapidly and sometimes chews the lapels of clothes. He may open the doors of neighbors' homes and likes to turn on water hoses at nearby homes. He is not afraid of dangerous high places and has been found trying to balance himself at the top of monkey bars and swing sets located in the playground behind the Franklin senior citizens' complex one block west of Maple at the corner of Main.

Do not attempt to restrain him when he is involved in these behaviors. Control his behaviors by providing him with a quiet space where he can calm down. He will not tell you if he is hurt. Michael cannot tell you his name, address, or phone number. Michael will repeatedly ask what your name is and your birth date. Those who consistently and repeatedly answer these questions will continue to hold his attention. Engaging in this repeated conversation allows Michael to calm down.

Michael has a laminated ID card sewn into the back pocket of his jeans, and his T-shirts have permanent-ink ID information printed on them at the lower-left back section. The eyelets of his running shoes have an ID tag affixed.

Michael may find his way to the wooded park section located at 760 Elm directly to the north of the Franklin senior citizens' complex. He has been found in the past playing with pine cones at this location. He is also attracted to the door chimes of the home at 1134 Maple. The intersection of Maple and Main is a high traffic area and located one block east of a curve in the road – Michael is sometimes lured to this location to watch for passing fire engines, ice-cream or garbage trucks.

Michael sleeps in the upstairs bedroom located in the northeast corner of our home. A yellow 'Occupant with Autism' decal is affixed to this window. During a storm, he would be found in the basement of our home.

Awareness options for individual families

Law enforcement professionals have indicated that entering emergency information into 911 systems is best done as a group, but individual families can also conduct an effective awareness campaign.

- Call the local police department to arrange a time to explain about autism and how to have emergency response information entered into the 911 or emergency system.

- For smaller departments or precincts of larger departments, ask that officers who regularly patrol a particular neighborhood visit the home.

- Ask to deliver the specific information at shift change or roll calls for police, fire, EMS, and hospital emergency room staff and store security.

Addressing elopement and misidentification issues by taking home safety precautions, identifying danger zones, alerting neighbors and emergency responders, considering ID wear or technology, teaching our kids appropriate social behavior, preparing and distributing information, and conducting public-awareness campaigns for our loved ones will become another, perhaps unanticipated, part of the job for parents and caregivers. But if it prevents even one unfortunate situation, and provides some peace of mind, it will be well worth it.

9

Victim and Law Enforcement Awareness for Persons with Autism and Advocates

Bullying and restraint in schools

We have addressed victim issues from a law enforcement perspective in Section One, but parents, advocates, and persons with autism are reporting a rise in incidents of teasing, torment, bullying, and poor restraint practices in schools. When these incidents occur, school administrators investigate and law enforcers may be called to respond. Understanding the precursors and circumstances of harassment and restraint and the methods used to identify and address them can help parents, educators, and all students enjoy a safer environment in schools.

Harassment, teasing, and bullying

Teasing and bullying are forms of harassment that can result in retaliation attempts by students with autism. When a student with autism or other disability has an outburst in school, it could be the student's lack of impulse control or an inappropriate emotional response. It could also be a reaction to bullying or teasing. Teachers and aides may miss the initial harassment of this student. They often see only the retaliation.

When questioned, the honest-till-it-hurts student with autism quickly confesses to the transgression. But the student with autism may not report the initial harassment. If he or she does, the bully goes into full denial. Bullies know when to remain silent. When it becomes one student's word against another's, the student with autism will often lack credibility as a reporter of facts. But his or her quick confession remains on the record. He or she may face suspension, expulsion, or criminal charges.

Parent and caregiver reports indicate a disturbing rise in cases where in response to teasing, torment and bullying the person with autism has made utterances or threats against persons or buildings or assaulted others. In particular, students with higher functioning autism or Asperger's Syndrome – some as young as six years old – have been arrested and/or expelled from school for making terroristic threats or for assault. When these responses lack any real intent other than making the harassment stop, it may be difficult to convince otherwise school officials, and law enforcement and criminal justice professionals who have zero tolerance for such acts.

Consider this report from one parent about her 16-year-old son who has autism and attends the regular-education high school:

> Despite preparations through Sam's Individualized Educational
> Plan, accommodations to have a 'safe' person available to him in all
> unstructured settings in the school were not in place. Sam was
> supposed to be able to go to this safe person whenever he needed help
> in a social situation he could not understand.
>
> On the third day of school, a student at Sam's lunchroom table
> began kicking him. When Sam became agitated, the teasing
> escalated. The other student began throwing french fries with
> ketchup on Sam's favorite shirt. Sam, obsessing on the idea that the
> ketchup would permanently ruin the shirt, became very upset. The
> other student, amused, wadded up a napkin and dipped it in ketchup.
> He then threw the napkin at Sam.

*Since Sam's only strategy for this situation was to go to a 'safe'
person and there was none to be found, Sam went after the other
student to try to make him stop throwing ketchup. The lunchroom
monitor did not see any of the previous behavior, but did see Sam go
after the other student. He and another lunchroom monitor
simultaneously tackled Sam, slammed his head into a plate of
ketchup on the table and then put him into a headlock. When they
got Sam to verbally agree to calm down, they released him.*

*Sam immediately lunged away from them toward the other
student who was laughing at him. When the monitors tried to grab
Sam, he took a swing at both of them. The monitors then tackled
Sam again, this time bringing him to the floor and sitting on him.
Again, they got him to verbally agree to calm down. Again, when
they released him, he tried to get away. They ended up dragging him
under headlock to the nurse's office at the school. She, being a
familiar person to him, was able to calm him down.*

*Now, Sam is charged with assaulting the other boy and the two
lunchroom monitors. The monitors, not knowing of his autism,
actually escalated Sam's agitation by holding him. The Juvenile
Court intake worker basically concluded that this is a violence-prone
youth who should probably be sent to a detention center. Admittedly,
he does look bad on paper.*

*However, those who know him best attest to his usually docile
manner. He is conscientious, reliable, hardworking, and gentle
spirited. He goes to great lengths to avoid trouble situations.
Unfortunately, other kids love to tease him because they know which
buttons to push for a reaction, and they know just when to stop so
that they don't get caught, but Sam doesn't.*

*I am so scared for my son. We hope for an understanding
District Attorney.*

Many people who are bullied will choose a place where there are no
witnesses to tell their tormenter off. Those bullied may utter threats that
they have no intention of carrying out, safe in the secrecy of their

threats and able to deny them to anyone else. The person with autism, too, may tell the bully what's on his or her mind with no intention at all of committing the act. But, the person with autism will verbally express his or her anger and frustration elsewhere without a care as to who may be listening. Denial? No, of course not, it was the righteous thing to do. The public verbal display, witnessed by many, only adds credibility to the belief by others that the person with autism will do what he or she says, or worse.

This exemplifies the ultimate criminal justice dilemma for those with autism: as victims or witnesses they lack credibility and their statements are not to be believed or accepted, but when in a situation of being an alleged perpetrator their statements become highly believable and acceptable. Fair justice? Should society and the criminal justice system have it both ways?

Harassment awareness

Teachers and parents should consider bullying, teasing, and harassment as they develop the indiMcGorry, P.D. (1995) 'Psychoeducation in first episode psychosis: A therapeutic process.' *Psychiatry 58*, 313–328.vidualized educational plan (IEP) for the student. Autism-awareness and antibullying informational sessions for peers, their parents, and school staff – from principals, teachers, aides, sports and leisure staff to custodial, food preparation, transportation, and school security staff or police liaison officer – should be part of any IEP for a student being educated in a general education environment. Not including these issues will leave the student with autism in a risky situation and may doom an otherwise good school program to failure.

When even seemingly innocent teasing happens, it should never be ignored. To root out and prevent bullying, teachers and school administrators must become more vigilant in the hallways, lunchrooms, playgrounds, and other places students spend unstructured, unmonitored time. This is not only a good practice – it's the law.

In a 25 July, 2000 joint Dear Colleague letter on Disability Based Harassment from the United States Department of Education's Office for Civil Rights (OCR), Assistant Secretary Norma V. Cantu and Office of Special Education and Rehabilitative Services (OSERS) Assistant Secretary Judith E. Heumann state that schools, colleges, universities, and other educational institutions have a responsibility to ensure equal educational opportunities for all students, including students with disabilities, based on Section 504 of the Rehabilitation Act of 1973 (Section 504), Title II of the Americans with Disabilities Act (Title II), which are enforced by the OCR. Disability harassment is a form of discrimination prohibited by Section 504 and Title II.

States and school districts also have a responsibility under Section 504, Title II, and the Individuals with Disabilities Education Act (IDEA), which is enforced by OSERS, to ensure that a free appropriate public education (FAPE) is made available to eligible students with disabilities. Disability harassment may result in a denial of FAPE under these statutes. Both Section 504 and Title II provide parents and students with grievance procedures and due process remedies at the local level. FAPE violations are also enforced by the OCR and OSERS' Office of Special Education Programs (OSEP).

Harassing conduct may also violate state and local civil rights, child abuse and criminal laws. Some of these laws may impose obligations on educational institutions to contact or coordinate with state or local agencies or police with respect to disability harassment in some cases. Failure to follow these procedures could result in action against an educational institution.

Disability harassment under Section 504 and Title II is intimidation or abusive behavior toward a student, based on disability, that creates a hostile environment within the institution's program or denies a student's participation in or receipt of benefits, services, or opportunities from the program. Harassing conduct may take many forms, including verbal acts and name-calling, as well as nonverbal behavior such as graphic and written statements or conduct that is physically threatening, harmful, or humiliating.

The following measures are ways to both prevent and eliminate harassment:

- Creating a campus environment that is aware of disability concerns and sensitive to disability harassment; weaving these issues into the curriculum or programs outside the classroom.

- Encouraging parents, students, employees, and community members to discuss disability harassment and to report it when they become aware of it.

- Widely publicizing antiharassment statements and procedures for handling complaints, because this information makes students and employees aware of what constitutes harassment, that such conduct is prohibited, that the institution will not tolerate such behavior, and that effective action – including disciplinary action, where appropriate – will be taken.

- Providing appropriate, up-to-date, and timely training for staff and students to recognize and handle potential harassment.

- Counseling both persons who have been harmed by harassment and persons who have been responsible for the harassment of others.

- Implementing monitoring programs to follow up on resolved issues of disability harassment.

- Regularly assessing and, as appropriate, modifying existing disability harassment policies and procedures for addressing the issue, to ensure effectiveness.

U.S. Secretary of Education Richard Riley has emphasized the importance of ensuring that schools are safe and free of harassment. Students cannot learn in an atmosphere of fear, intimidation, or ridicule. For students with disabilities, harassment can inflict severe harm (United States Department of Education 2000).

Disability harassment is preventable and cannot be tolerated. Schools, colleges, and universities should address the issue of disability harassment not just when but also *before* incidents occur.

Liza Little, PsyD, R.N., also offers suggestions and questions for parents and educators who are concerned with disability harassment, in her article 'Peer Victimization of Children with AS and NLD,' (Little 2000, p.6):

- Schools need to be educated and held responsible for protecting your child.

- Does your school have a bully prevention program? If not, advocate for one.

- Does your child's teacher understand the high risk for peer victimization your child may have? Is he or she trained to address this with students and monitor it carefully?

- Do bus drivers and recess monitors understand that your child's AS or NLD increases their chance for difficulties? Are there clear rules for reporting bullying behavior?

- Does the school have systems in place for monitoring children at risk and protecting them?

- Follow up on your child's complaints of victimization and don't expect your child to know how to negotiate with bullies. Are perpetrators being educated and facing consequences?

- Initiate a buddy system for your child; school professionals may also help you do this.

Restraint

Applying techniques of restraint is commonly known as *crisis prevention*. In addition to law enforcement professionals, those who work with children and adults with autism may find it necessary to restrain them when their behaviors escalate into situations where they may harm themselves or others. It may be too late for positive supports when the student is choking a classmate or kicking the teacher. No one should have to be afraid of being hurt at school.

But parents and advocates have reported incidents where persons who have received inadequate training on how and when crisis interventions should be used are physically restraining students with ASD. Reportedly, proper training techniques are being diluted through the practice of second- and third-generation training conducted by unqualified trainers. Other reports indicate that restraint is being used solely for compliance – for instance, to get the child to do their schoolwork or get on a bus. Even with the best intentions, restraint has the potential for abuse when practiced by those who lack the training, ability, or good judgment to use it.

All concerned parents, advocates, educators, and care professionals must ensure that anyone using crisis intervention receives proper, quality instruction on its physical techniques and the appropriate situations in which to use them. Reporting and training methods for those who use restraint should be under constant review. Videotaping all interventions can increase the professionalism of those who intervene, by protecting against allegations of abuse, documenting when it goes wrong, and providing models for training.

Currently there is no federal regulation regulating the use of restraints in schools and in day care and day treatment facilities. However, restraint is federally regulated for use in mental health facilities, habilitation centers, and psychiatric wards. A physician must order the restraints, and nursing staff personnel must be present and face to face with the person being restrained. A person cannot be restrained or secluded for more than twenty minutes at a time, unless ordered by a physician. Mechanical restraints must be removed each hour for at least five minutes.

Some states do have legislation in place regulating the use of restraint and seclusion in schools and day care centers. Massachusetts recently passed legislation providing guidance in training, administration, and duration of restraint/seclusion in schools. Illinois recently declared a moratorium on the use of restraint/seclusion due to the death of a student. This moratorium will be lifted when legislation has been passed and regulations regarding restraint have been written and disseminated to schools. Parents and caregivers should check with their state to see if such legislation exists and regulations have been written that guide the use of restraint. Another opportunity exists for being involved in the process of improving the lives of people with autism by involving legislators, advocates, and people with autism in these efforts.

Techniques of restraint can be reviewed in the discussion in Chapter 2, under 'Response.'

Law enforcement recognition and response

Developing at an early age the law enforcement awareness of students with autism can broaden their understanding of the role of law enforcement professionals. A person's ability to differentiate a law enforcement professional from a stranger is an essential lifetime element for personal safety and success in the community. Programs are needed that enable children and adults with autism to identify police officers as persons they can trust when problems are experienced.

These formal or informal programs can be a part of any social-awareness program for a student with autism. Community policing, school liaison, and training officers can provide input on basic law enforcement awareness and safety information for development into the curriculum. Some points to consider:

- Provide opportunities for students to become familiar with officers as members of the community.

- Practice interactions through mock interviews.

- Teach how to respond appropriately to basic questions and requests such as giving names, addresses, and phone numbers or presenting an identification card.

- Teach appropriate ways to call for emergency help.

Students with autism may need extra preparation to avoid becoming a victim or an alleged accomplice:

- Having autism is not an excuse for doing something wrong.

- If another person commits a crime in your presence, leave the area and call the police.

- Don't do something just because a friend says it's OK.

Improving contacts with the police

Individuals who are fully or semi-independent in the community have reported difficulties when they suddenly encounter a law enforcement professional. Adults with autism say that they often experience anxiety and fear when they even think about having these interactions. They fear misunderstandings and heavy scrutiny. Their experiences give them good reasons for this fear. Adults with autism have described encounters with police who roughed up the person when he or she failed to respond verbally during a seizure episode; of being searched and threatened by police looking for a similarly dressed suspect; of being ejected from a building and a public bus for being accompanied by a support dog; and of being searched by police who believed that the person was high on drugs. The common denominator in all of these incidents was a display of the behaviors and characteristics of autism to law enforcers who could not recognize and respond to them.

In spite of increasing efforts to make law enforcers aware, it is a reasonable and safe assumption that most law enforcement professionals are *not yet* trained to recognize and respond to a person with autism. While it is not legally necessary to identify oneself as having a disability, to ensure safety in the community and when traveling it may be advisable to do so.

Law enforcers have a tough job to do. Even with the best of training, they too may experience anxiety and fear in new situations. There is a fear of the unknown when they come across such a variety of people each day. They don't know their intentions. They don't know how some people will react to them. Law enforcers have described their daily experience as hours of routine interspersed with minutes of high anxiety whenever they approach people they do not know. Officer injury and deaths resulting from these never ordinary interactions are real reasons for their heightened sense of fear. Without information or training to the contrary, law enforcers will remain suspicious when they encounter persons whose behavior is not easily explained.

There is only so much that a law enforcer can learn about autism from a parent, advocate, or informational handout or videotape. Direct communication between those with autism and law enforcers is recommended for any workshop. Advocacy organizations can develop programs or regular meetings where adults with autism and law-enforcers can meet to discuss issues. The law enforcement professionals should be asked to address these meetings to explain the role of law enforcement, offer safety tips and information on how to report a crime, and conduct question-and-answer sessions about ways a person with autism can better interact with officers.

While there are adolescents and adults on the spectrum who can recognize and avoid unfortunate situations, there are others who cannot. It can only be of assistance to the latter if others become involved in these campaigns. They can also get valuable advice directly from law enforcement professionals and develop personal contacts that may become very useful.

Independent persons with autism often ask about what they can do when approached by law enforcement professionals. Law enforcers have suggested proper identification – a driver's license, passport, state identification card, and a prepared handout that includes information that the person has autism and may not understand their legal rights, explains behaviors that may appear suspicious, and gives any critical medical information and phone numbers for an advocate or law enforcement contact person.

Law enforcers also suggest keeping the following in mind:

- Do not attempt to flee.

- Do not make sudden movements.

- Try to remain calm.

- Verbally let officer know you have autism. If nonverbal, use alternative communication, such as simple sign language, to indicate the need to write or to present an information card.

- If unable to answer questions, consider the use of a generic or person-specific autism information card.

- Obtain permission or signal intentions before reaching into coat or pants pocket.

- Ask officer to contact an advocate, if necessary.

- For the best protection of all involved, the person with autism who has been arrested should, either verbally or through an information card, invoke the right to remain silent and ask to be represented by an attorney.

- If you are a victim or are reporting a crime, you do not need to have an attorney present to speak to the police, but you may want the police to contact a family member, advocate, or friend who can help you through the interview process.

Travel safety tips

Customs, immigration and security checkpoints

From common everyday trips in the community to international travel, persons with autism will have to prepare for encounters with law enforcers. Adults with autism have reported difficulties at international border crossings. In one case, a person with autism was detained, and then committed to an asylum by customs and immigration officials who mistook the person for being psychotic.

Questioning and observation are predictable procedures at international borders and at airport, building, and event security checkpoints. Persons with autism should seek advice from and present autism information to travel agents, airline, train, bus, or other transportation personnel. Before crossing international borders, persons with disabilities should inquire about any procedures that customs and immigration use.

Carry written information in all appropriate languages about autism to present at airport security, customs and immigration checkpoints, and anywhere the situation calls for. Before traveling, persons with autism and companions should consider obtaining a letter from their local law enforcement agency, community health agency, a doctor, or advocacy organization that clearly identifies the person, offers a phone contact number, and states in simple terms that the person's behavior should not be misunderstood as necessarily criminal in nature.

Avoiding victimization

Unfortunately, citizens with autism may need to take extra precautions to avoid becoming a victim of street crime. A robber, for instance, will look for persons who appear to be unfamiliar with or new to their surroundings. They will notice those who may dawdle or move slowly or too quickly. The criminally bent individual becomes skilled at finding the perfect victim from those who appear timid, who wear clothes that are unusual to the area, who may speak with an accent, who are people-watchers who gawk, who have no eye contact or unusually long eye contact, who appear overly friendly, or whose appearance or behavior is different from that of the crowd.

These criminal individuals will follow their selected victim to see if they go to an area away from close scrutiny – for instance, a wooded area, a restroom, parking structure, alley, or dead-end walkway. Robbers will quickly approach, state that they have a weapon or produce one, and demand money or belongings. If caught in this situation, the victim should not resist. The victim should give the robbers what they want, make sure they have departed the area, and then call the police.

To avoid victimization:

- Travel in a group.
- Hire a guide or reliable person to accompany the group.
- Make sure others know your whereabouts.
- Avoid unknown areas during 'off hours'.
- Do not wander or explore off the beaten path.

10

Advocacy for Offenders
with Autism Spectrum Disorders

Autism awareness in the criminal justice system

Parents work hard to prepare their children for successful, productive lives that include their right to self-determination and access to the community. The lives of those with autism who are able to achieve this success through their own hard work and the help and understanding of others are celebrated. And they should be.

Then there are the sobering realities for some: adolescents and adults who learn to self-medicate with alcohol and street drugs; the poor choices in friends that some make; the depression autism can bring; being brought up in an environment of crime. While there is no reason to believe that a person with autism is more likely to commit a criminal offense than anyone else, some persons with autism have committed, been charged with, and convicted of crimes.

Reports indicate that these crimes are often a result of the person's attempts to end harassment, bullying, or teasing by others or to express sexual curiosity. Some find their way through unlocked doors and are charged with entering occupied dwellings. Attempts at making friends can be seen as stalking. They may become accomplices to others who take criminal advantage of their guilelessness and technical skills. Some commit violent acts.

We have discussed offender trends and mitigating factors in Section One but the results of even the most guileless acts of a person with autism can result in needless feelings of fear, intimidation, and helplessness by the victim and law enforcement scrutiny of often the best preparations, precautions, and actions that parents and caregivers may take.

The many undiagnosed cases on the higher-functioning end of the spectrum leave some with inappropriate social awareness and without access to educational opportunities that might have prevented them from getting involved in criminal activities. Indeed, it is often the case that a person receives a first or accurate diagnosis as a result of the scrutiny of the criminal justice system. Whether the diagnosis came as a result of the incident or not, it can be difficult to present ASD as a mitigating factor in a criminal case.

When laws have been broken and others victimized, the person's fate will be in the hands of criminal justice professionals who are usually misinformed and ignorant about autism. A good defense attorney who understands autism or is willing to try will be hard to come by. Prosecutors may look at autism as another defense ploy for leniency.

Pat Hawk, a Florida-based advocate for people with developmental disabilities, president of the Autism Society of Marion County, and mom of a son with autism, stated that the problem with offender issues is that the parents, guardians, and advocates treat it like a hot potato.

> If over 1000 disabled kids are incarcerated in Florida alone each year, wouldn't one expect a few hundred advocates to come out of that experience? But nope, everyone runs for cover at the earliest possible time. Nothing much is done to improve the situation, and then it happens again.

> We need to get this out of being a shame-based issue to one that needs advocating. We must become proactive and educate those willing to listen. Parents need to know that if they have a developmentally disabled child incarceration is highly likely to happen and they need to be prepared to climb the steps of the justice system. If we were already criminals, dealing with the justice system would be much easier for us. We would be more informed,

more prepared, and would know all the tricks. (Personal communication, 2001)

Autism, as a condition in the life of an individual, should be considered
a mitigating factor during every part of the criminal justice process. But
the case can be made only when those professionals are aware of the
defendant's autism. Families, advocates, and defense attorneys will need
to conduct autism-awareness campaigns that are sensitive to the needs
of the victim, the criminal justice system, and the offender with autism.
In all cases, individuals with autism and their families will need the
support and understanding of autism advocates. Advocates must also
bear in mind the plight and needs of the victim and seek to learn about
their feelings and understanding of autism.

Those who do not understand the implications of their acts and are
unable to learn how to avoid them in the future will be at risk of receiving habitual-offender punishments. They will be incarcerated in prisons
or institutions that are ill equipped to deal with an offender with
autism. Once there, they often fall prey to other inmates. They will find
good-time credits hard to come by and serve longer sentences. Advocates unfamiliar with the criminal justice system will be able to offer
little support. Fair justice will be hard to find. This is often the sad
reality for those with autism and their families when they become
involved with the criminal justice system.

In this section we look at the criminal justice issues that can affect
our loved ones with autism.

Court proceedings

Competency hearings

Those charged with offenses may be examined for competency as the
criminal case proceeds. An appropriate psychiatric expert will examine
the defendant for competency. Those working for the prosecution or
police are commonly called forensic experts. If the defendant is found
to be incompetent to assist in his or her defense or unable to form the
necessary criminal intent to commit the crimes he or she was charged
with, the court may remand the defendant to a state or private facility

where he or she may be kept until it is decided that he or she is no longer a threat to society. The judge will determine the facility.

Trial

If the person is found competent, a trial will be set. The issue of intent and all other issues may be argued at trial. A defense attorney may decide on a defense based on competence or mental defect. In such cases, if found innocent because of these reasons, the defendant, once again, will be remanded by a judge to an appropriate facility until he or she is no longer a threat to society.

A jury or judge may find a defendant guilty of the crime. Or, of course, the defendant may be found innocent and set free. If found guilty, a defendant's competency, intent, and other mitigating factors will be brought up during sentencing.

Diagnosis, intent and mitigating factors

There will be situations where it is clear that the person with autism has committed a crime and may very well be deemed as competent to assist in his or her defense. For such persons, it will become an issue of intent. Defense attorneys and prosecutors through the testimony of psychiatric experts often argue intent in court. It will become their job to make a judge or jury aware of any mitigating factors that are linked to the crime, such as a person's autism. When experts, lawyers, and jurists are unfamiliar with autism and its wide spectrum of severity, a defendant's recall of the facts, for example, may lead one to believe that he or she can form the necessary intent to commit the criminal act. The apparent clear understanding in association with the appearance of a lack of remorse may be an erroneous show of intent. For example, a young man with Asperger's syndrome was involved in an act of arson with three other boys. They acted remorseful in court; this boy didn't seem to care, so he was locked up.

There are cases where defense attorneys and experts who are trying to determine intent first diagnose autism in the offender as a result of the heavy scrutiny of their background. Psychiatric experts for prosecutors may disagree with the findings or argue that it does not have an effect on intent. But the fact remains that those on the higher-functioning end of the spectrum, especially those diagnosed with Asperger's syndrome (AS) are much more difficult to diagnose, may have a family background of denial of disability, or may have been misdiagnosed. AS diagnosis is becoming more common as better information and diagnostic tools surface and the stigma attached to the autism spectrum lessens. Criminal justice professionals will need to become aware of the higher rate of diagnosis of those with AS and consider the new diagnosis, or any diagnosis, as a mitigating factor and not necessarily a defense ploy for leniency.

Whenever someone is found guilty of an offense, advocates will need to guard carefully against a conviction based on evidence that is solely linked to the person's autism. It may very well be that the person with autism, typically misunderstood and with no criminal intent, perpetrated a criminal act inadvertently. Likewise, autism itself cannot be expected to exonerate someone of his or her criminal responsibility. If that were the case, advocating for full community inclusion and self-determination would become a difficult prospect. There remains the possibility that the person did intend to do what he or she was charged with. While advocates may argue over the issue of whether any person with autism can form criminal intent, they will need to understand that others will calculate intent on a case-by-case basis.

To find justice for victim and offender alike, psychiatric and psychological experts, department of corrections pre-sentence investigators, defense attorneys, prosecutors, and judges may seek input from autism advocates. Advocates with influence are fair, objective, and known to treat each case individually.

The victim

How the victim feels about the offender and disability will have a strong bearing on the outcome of justice. For example, the nonverbal person who enters an occupied home, goes to the refrigerator, drinks every soft drink found, and then leaves may find a completely different level of understanding from the victim than the odd, unusually dressed, higher-functioning man who stands in waiting outside a young woman's house as she comes home from work. The victim's levels of disability acceptance and understanding may be at opposite ends.

Explaining the disability to the victim will become the responsibility of advocates, law enforcers, and criminal justice professionals. Proactive public awareness can be a very effective tool when engaged with the victim in dispelling disability myths, stigmas and misinformation. Objective advocates can prepare to address this issue beforehand through partnerships with and advice from criminal justice professionals, community mental health professionals, and victim's rights advocates.

Sentencing

Incidents involving persons with autism as offenders are not at an epidemic stage but occur with enough frequency that they warrant the attention of advocacy organizations. Despite the best effort that advocates can muster or when the punishment fits the crime, some with autism may find themselves sent to correctional facilities to serve their time.

Habitual offender laws – three strikes and you're out

Because of their limited ability to learn from their mistakes and their tendency to repeat actions, those with ASD may become involved in repeat occurrences of nonviolent misdemeanors or felonies. They may also be unable to access appropriate services from any public system and must rely on advocates who sometimes fail to monitor or correct inaccurate records. Subsequently, they may find themselves falling into the ugly cracks of habitual offender statutes that were designed to identify and isolate criminal offenders who *choose* a life of crime, not those who are unable by nature and circumstances to escape from one. When convicted, advocates and defense attorneys should take great care in making sure that the permanent record contains language related to the person's disability that can help guard against their becoming labeled a habitual offender.

Correctional facilities

With most offenders, the punishment should fit the crime. For those with autism, the punishment may need to fit the offender.

Dr. Joan Petersilia, a criminology professor at the University of California-Irvine and a world-renowned expert and advocate for the legal rights of those with developmental disabilities, pled the case for consideration of the needs of this population in her testimony at a session of the California state legislature.

> Once in jail or prison, other inmates often victimize them. Because of their cognitive limitations, they are likely to have a difficult time understanding jail and prison rules and may spend much time in segregation – which limits their work opportunities, and hence 'good-time' credits and early release. Because [California] has few specialized rehabilitation or parole programs for reintegrating people with developmental disabilities once they are released, their entrance into the revolving-door cycle of prison to parole and back to prison is predictable. At $22,000.00 per year per inmate, such a scenario should offend our cost consciousness as well as our sense of equal justice (Petersilia 2000 p.11).

Incarceration in a typical prison would almost certainly put a person with autism at risk and vulnerable to abuse from other inmates. Such incarceration could be considered cruel and unusual punishment. If the person with autism is sentenced to prison or sent to a state mental-health facility, she or he need to maintain her or his civil rights and legal access to services. Advocates must ensure that persons with autism are housed in an appropriate facility and see that they receive appropriate services whenever and wherever they are incarcerated. Alternatives to prison should be considered, including secured residential facilities, electronic monitoring, and, if possible, diversion programs.

Disability courts and diversion programs

> The Broward County, Florida disability or 'mental health' court began operating on June 16, 1997 and is believed to be the first of its kind in the U.S. Established to handle misdemeanor court cases involving individuals with disabilities, the court is set up to quickly resolve such cases and divert the individuals away from jails and into appropriate treatment programs.
>
> The county appointed a judge familiar with disability issues who expedites cases on the same day as or the day after the initial arrest. The court has the authority to divert individuals into in- or outpatient treatment, to release them, or to revoke conditional discharges when individuals do not comply with treatment plans. Several similar courts are now in operation in the U.S. (National Alliance for the Mentally Ill 1997)

Disability courts have been established or are being formed in some jurisdictions across the United States and offer diversion options for offenders with autism. Diversion is a program to allow offenders who are not believed to be repeat offenders to have a second chance. Advocates seeking fair justice for those with autism should keep in mind diversion programs that exist for alcohol and drug abusers. If the criminal justice system can find many ways to divert offenders who often choose this path in life, can it not also find diversion useful for those with disabilities who have no choice in theirs? For example, a diversion for a convicted drunk driver might be completion of a court-ordered alcohol detoxification program and six months' community service such as cleaning highways or working with victims of accidents. A diversion program for a person with autism who has been convicted of misdemeanor assault, stalking, or indecent exposure might be court-ordered counseling to help him or her better understand and control his or her aggression, along with an appropriate community service. In both cases, the court would monitor the offender's progress. If successful, the charges would not appear on the person's permanent record.

Advocates can work with their local criminal justice professionals to help them better understand the offender with autism and the mitigating factors that the condition may bring to the situation. Working for the creation of disability courts and diversion programs for offenders with autism offers some of the best hopes for fair justice for our loved ones. Advocates will find useful information about forming these partnerships in the next chapter under 'Community Agency Collaborations.'

11

Collaborative Autism-Awareness Campaigns

Community policing

Community policing is a philosophy that is embraced by law enforcement agencies in many areas of the world. The commitment to this philosophy is put into practice by law enforcement agencies in the form of increased attention to the voices of community members. Groups that possess knowledge which helps law enforcers understand and address unique issues of concern, and improve training, procedures, response, and investigative techniques are considered an asset to modern law enforcement agencies.

Bringing public awareness of autism to the community at large has long been a concern for advocates. Organized public-awareness and education campaigns are, quite simply, efforts that allow others to understand and make reasonable accommodations for our loved ones. Law enforcement professionals, therefore, should be considered a target audience for any organized public-awareness campaign.

The role of a national advocacy organization

Autism-awareness campaigns for law enforcement are best described as grass-roots partnerships that address the needs of both communities.

National and regional autism organizations should make a commitment to become credible, stable resources for law enforcement agencies and local advocates. While leadership may change in these organizations, good programs will continue to thrive. Those organizations that make law enforcement awareness a permanent agenda item can be most helpful when they embrace curriculum and educational materials that are uniform yet flexible enough to be adapted for local use.

Plan of action

Law enforcement awareness can be successfully accomplished by national autism advocacy organizations that consider the following plans of action:

- Identify potential partners within national law enforcement agencies and criminal justice organizations and legislators who can provide credibility for these campaigns.

- Form a permanent committee of advocates and law enforcement, emergency service, and criminal justice members to review, select, and recommend curriculum.

- Organize an initial national workshop for law enforcement and emergency service supervisors and trainers and local autism advocates.

- Develop promotional materials for use at local, regional, and national law enforcement conferences, and for print, television, and radio media publicity

- Disseminate the availability of curriculum and promotional materials to local advocacy organizations.

- Create and maintain a database for law enforcement referrals to local advocacy agencies and to track, list, and disseminate upcoming workshop information to law enforcement and emergency services, the media, and educational and governmental institutions.

Grass-roots campaigns

The format of grass-roots campaigns can vary from informal presentations at shift change or roll-call briefings, to more formal workshops or train-the-trainers sessions. Local advocates can organize a successful first-time workshop by adopting the following plan of action:

Who

- Contact the local sheriff's office, chief of police, and training-unit officers and determine the best time and date.

- Invite police school resource and child abuse officers and representatives from area fire departments, emergency medical services, hospital emergency rooms, social service and child welfare agencies, and mall and event security companies.

- Invite concerned persons with autism, parents, and caregivers.

- Invite educators, adult care providers, community health agency professionals, legislators, and criminal justice professionals.

- Invite Alzheimer's disease, mental retardation, mental illness, and other physical- and intellectual-disability advocacy organizations with similar concerns.

When

- At time and date acceptable to main audience.

- Consider repeating session or modified version for same evening.

- Develop a flyer that can be distributed to target audiences.

- If appropriate, develop a press release and give at least six weeks' notice to local print, radio and television media.

Where

- Select a comfortable venue that is acceptable to audience.
- Provide refreshments.

What

- Outline the main points of recommended curriculum:
    1. basic autism recognition and response
    2. for first-responders: de-escalation, misidentification, elopement, and custody
    3. for investigators: interview/interrogation, victim/witness
    4. avoid lawsuits and provide for safety of all concerned
- Use appropriate video presentations.
- If possible, involve persons with autism.
- Organize a panel to discuss the general concerns of both populations that includes persons with autism, parents, and law enforcement representatives.
- Provide written materials, such as:
    1. a sample parent/caregiver handout for law enforcers and first-responders (see Chapter 2)
    2. complete copies of recommended curriculum
    3. a recognition and response handout (see below)
    4. appropriate articles and news clips
    5. autism brochures
    6. local contact phone numbers for autism advocates
    7. resource list of related products, videos, curriculum and agencies.

Why

- To educate key community service personnel.

- To develop police contacts who can help solve problem issues as they arise.

- To develop contacts among law enforcement professionals who can present on police awareness in classrooms, group homes, work places, and Autism Society meetings.

- To develop contacts for future workshops and training sessions within police academies, training units, colleges, and universities that provide curriculum, in-service, and certification courses for recruits and veterans.

- To develop contacts for referrals to other agencies.

- To become reliable resources of autism information for law enforcement and emergency service agencies.

The presenters

- Consider using recognized speakers or presenters who are familiar with the material and with public speaking.

- Ask local law enforcement, fire, and EMS agencies to send a representative who can speak about their services.

- Invite manufacturers and security companies to briefly present about or display related products and services.

- The more varied the speaker list, the more interest will be generated.

Tips for first-time presenters:

- Rehearse presentation several times. Videotape rehearsals, if possible.

- Presenters are hosts and guides to a local audience that is unfamiliar with autism. To be effective:

1. use terms and language that are understandable
2. keep in mind the point of view of law enforcement professionals
3. be objective
4. refer often to the curriculum and materials
5. identify the numbers of local families affected by autism
6. personalize the message: if possible, use local stories and anecdotes
7. or refer to news clippings or published stories for real life examples
8. seek input and ask questions of audience often.

Recognition and response handout

The following is a sample handout for a law enforcement workshop. It is based on the handout presented in *Educating the Public and Law Enforcement* (Debbaudt 1996).

Law enforcement responders may unexpectedly encounter or be asked to find a person with autism. Recognizing the behavior symptoms and knowing contact approaches can minimize situations of risk – risk of victimization of the person with autism, and risk to the interveners.

Recognizing persons with autism

- May be nonverbal (approximately 50 per cent of this population is nonverbal), or may only repeat what is said to them; may communicate with sign language or picture cards or use gestures and pointing.

- May not respond to 'Stop' command, may run or move away when approached, may cover ears and look away constantly.

- May have seizure disorder that is not apparent to responder.

- May toe-walk, have pigeon-toed gait or running style.

- May appear as high on drugs, drunk, or having a psychotic episode.

- May react to sudden changes in routine or to sensory input – for example, lights, sirens, canine partners, odors – with escalation of repetitive behavior, such as pacing, hand-flapping, hand-twirling, hitting self, screaming (temper tantrums are an expected response to fear, confusion, or frustration as an effort to stop the stimuli).

- May attempt to present an autism information card; may wear medical alert jewelry or have information sewn or imprinted on clothes or on nonpermanent tattoo.

- May not recognize danger or hurt; may possess weak help-seeking skills; may not be able to distinguish between minor and serious problems; may not know where/how to get help for problems; may not be able to give important information or be able to answer questions.

- May not recognize police vehicle, badge, or uniform or understand what is expected of them if they do.

- May have difficulty recognizing and repairing breakdowns in communication, such as asking for clarification or responding to a request for clarification; may not understand or accept your statements or answers.

- May appear argumentative, stubborn, or belligerent; may say 'No!' in response to all questions; may ask 'Why?' incessantly.

- May repeat exactly what you say.

- Will have difficulty interpreting body language, such as command presence or defensive posture, or facial expressions, such as raised eyebrows, rolling eyes, smiles, and frowns, and have difficulty recognizing jokes, teasing, and verbal/nonverbal emotional responses.

- May be poor listeners: may not seem to care what you have to say; their lack of eye contact may give you the feeling they aren't listening or have something to hide.

- May have passive, monotone voices with unusual pronunciations; often sound computer-like; will have difficulty using the correct volume for the situation.

- May have difficulty judging personal space; may stand too close or too far away; may not differentiate different body parts; may stare at you or present atypical fixed gaze.

- May perseverate on favorite topic when uncomfortable in the form of repeated questions – for example, What if? What's your name? – arguments, or apparent ramblings about favorite sports teams, train, bus, or plane schedules, city names.

- May have difficulty in seeing things from a different point of view; may have difficulty predicting other persons' reaction to them.

COLLABORATIVE AUTISM-AWARENESS CAMPAIGNS

- Are usually very honest, sometimes too honest; have behaviors limiting credibility with others but do not or ably tell lies; often very blunt, not tactful.

Suggested responses

During law enforcement patrol situations or encounters with persons with autism, the following responses should be considered:

- Talk in direct, short phrases, such as 'Stand up now. Go to the car.'

- Allow for delayed responses to questions or directions/commands.

- Avoid literal expressions and random comments, such as 'give my eye teeth to know', 'what's up your sleeve?', 'are you pulling my leg?', 'spread eagle', 'you think it's cool?'

- Talk calmly and/or repeat. Talking louder will not help understanding. Model calming body language, slow breathing, hands low.

- Person may not understand your defensive posture/body language; may continue to invade your space. Use low gestures for attention; avoid rapid pointing or waving; tell person you are not going to hurt them.

- Avoid behaviors and language that may appear threatening.

- Look and wait for response and/or eye contact; when comfortable, ask to 'look at me'; don't interpret limited eye contact as deceit or disrespect.

- If possible, avoid touching the person, especially near shoulders or face; avoid standing too near or behind; avoid stopping repetitive behaviors unless self-injurious or risk of injury to yourself or others.

- Evaluate for injury; person may not ask for help or show any indications of pain, even though injury seems apparent.

- Examine for presence of medical alert jewelry or tags; person may have seizure disorder.

- Be aware of person's self-protective responses to even usual lights, sounds, touch, orders, animals.

- If possible, turn off sirens and flashing lights and remove canine partners or other sensory stimulation from scene.

- If person's behavior escalates, maintain a safe distance until any inappropriate behaviors lessen, but remain alert to the possibility of outbursts or impulsive acts.

- Consider use of sign language, or picture or phrase books.

- If you take an individual into custody and even remotely suspect the person may have an autistic spectrum disorder, to reduce the risk of abuse and/or injury, ask jail authorities to segregate the individual and not to place them in the general incarcerated population before a mental health professional has evaluated them.

Community agency collaborations

Autism advocates can also make a difference when they become active participants in collaborative efforts to develop programs that address victim and offender issues. Criminal justice task forces exist at local, state, and national levels that exchange disability information regularly. These proactive collaborations have spawned comprehensive workshops that develop disability awareness, sensitivity, and a higher level of understanding within the disabilities, law enforcement, criminal justice, education, and community health communities. Advocates who offer autism recognition, response, and awareness to these collaborations stand the best chance for developing contacts in the criminal justice community. Task forces, for instance, can also be instrumental in the development of disability courts programs that divert offenders with disabilities away from prison sentences and into appropriate sentencing options.

One example of a successful partnership is a coalition developed by the Detroit-Wayne County Community Mental Health Agency (D-WCCMHA) and the Michigan chapter of Alliance for the Mentally Ill (AMI). Agencies as diverse as the Detroit Police Department, Michigan State Police, Wayne County Sheriff's Department, Wayne County Prosecutors Office, and the Michigan Department of Corrections have been meeting on a regular basis for the past seven years with hospital psychiatric emergency service providers; with advocates for autism, mental retardation, mental illness, Alzheimer's disease, the deaf community, adult care facilities, and homeless persons; with judges; and with many others. These meetings are designed to increase community awareness and acknowledgment of persons with mental illness and developmental disabilities who are in crisis (Debbaudt 2000b).

One by-product of this collaboration was the creation of a bi-monthly, two-day, 16-hour law enforcement and criminal justice training workshop, 'Effectively Working with Persons with Mental Illness and Developmental Disabilities'. The workshop allows law enforcement and criminal justice professionals to increase their knowledge of those with disabilities, become familiar with accessing services and support from the community mental health system, become sensitive to the needs and experiences of families and individuals with disabilities, and learn ways to deal effectively with them.

The significance of these workshops shouldn't be lost on autism advocates. They are not only wonderful opportunities to address a varied audience of key community service personnel, they can allow advocates to identify those professionals who have a personal connection to autism. It has been the personal experience of the author to identify law enforcers who are parents and siblings of those with autism at these workshops by merely asking at the onset of a presentation if anyone knows someone with autism. Contacts made at these workshops have opened the doors for other autism-specific awareness workshops – for example, a region-wide series for Michigan Department of Corrections probation and parole officers.

Diversion for offenders can often take place by utilizing contacts. With one phone call, contacts have been able to respond to calls for help from an offender's family by educating other criminal justice professionals that advocates would never have had access to. They aren't contacts until you use them. Like it or not, this is how the system often works.

Autism advocates involved in these coalitions will also become more educated to the needs of other disability groups and the law enforcement and criminal justice systems. The contacts and education become invaluable when advocating for families in need. Teaming up with Alzheimer's advocates on the issue of elopement, for example, can be a more effective way of getting action and understanding from a local law enforcement agency. A phone call to a hospital emergency room psychiatric-intake specialist is often all an advocate needs to get autism on his or her workshop agenda. Need someone to come to court or to help counsel an autism family in need? Call your contact from the Alliance for the Mentally Ill. Cognitive issues awareness for a school system? Buddy up with your friend from the deaf advocacy community. Need disabilities courts legislation passed? These are the letter writers. These contacts can help get the word out.

Advocates anywhere can inquire at their county or provincial governmental health agency about becoming involved in these projects. There are many projects across the country, and autism advocates are rare. If the collaboration does not yet exist, an autism advocacy group can work to organize one. There are many willing partners. Participation in these collaborations can be time-consuming, but for advocacy groups who have decided to permanently address the issue of law enforcement and criminal justice awareness of autism, they can be well worth the effort.

Autism-specific awareness

The tools of autism awareness

Autism advocacy groups can also address the issue by developing their own statewide program. A fine example of this is the Autism Society of South Carolina. Through their Autism and Informed Response program, complete with video and curriculum, they have been able to access over 2,000 law enforcement, fire, and emergency first-responders during training sessions and have identified local advocates throughout their state who are using the materials to conduct training in their communities.

Singular efforts by advocates resulted in first-ever projects: the *Autism Awareness Video for Law Enforcement/Community Service Personnel* (Swift 1998) and the Maryland Police and Correctional Training Commissions curriculum, *Why Law Enforcement Needs To Recognize Autism* (MPCTC 1999).

Judy Swift, a Harrisburg, Pennsylvania-based advocate, film producer, and mom of a spectrum child, was able to see her idea for a video through by organizing a development team. She found funding sources and recruited topnotch news production volunteers. The video is now in wide circulation throughout the United States as a law enforcement training tool and won the Autism Society of America's Excellence in Media award for 1999 (Debbaudt 2001).

In late 1998, Lisa Mathews, a Maryland mom of three boys with autism, decided to do something about law enforcement awareness. Her single-handed, persistent letter-writing and phone campaign to Maryland's top law enforcer, Governor Parris Glendening, paid off with a letter of referral to the MPCTC. Within three months, the MPCTC hired Dr. Darla Rothman as a curriculum specialist. Her first assignment: create a training curriculum about autism. The curriculum is the first, and only, autism-specific curriculum developed by a law enforcement agency and is used by law enforcement training units throughout the country as a model and reference source (Debbaudt 2001).

A model local campaign

The Autism Society of America chapter in Greater Orlando, Florida ,has used the tools well. Donna Lorman, the chapter president in 1999, began a campaign that will result in every Orange County Sheriff's Department officer receiving autism-specific training by the end of 2002. She understood the value of developing a contact person within the department. Donna first explained the importance of the issue to a lieutenant at the Sheriff's Department who agreed to work with the group. Initially, every sworn officer viewed Judy Swift's awareness video. Then she organized a 2001 train-the-trainer workshop utilizing the MPCTC autism curriculum. The trainers will begin training sessions in 2002 for their entire work force.

By-products from this campaign? Autism advocates have manned an awareness table at police functions. The Sheriff's Department set up an awareness booth at an autism day at an Orlando theme park. A side project began: judo training for kids with autism taught by off-duty deputies. The Sheriff's Department is considering an autism-specific radio code that will provide for better first responses.

Law enforcement awareness campaigns are often conducted by autism advocates in reaction to a traumatic event that occurred in a local community. But they will work best when they are credible, well-planned, and organized proactive campaigns that are not considered to be onetime efforts. The intended outcome of first-time workshops is to develop a permanent partnership with key agencies in the community, identify opportunities for a wider audience, identify the needs and concerns of the law enforcement community, identify through feedback any barriers to two-way communication, and develop effective ways to work through them. One law enforcement veteran was heard to comment after attending a workshop that he wished he had had the training earlier on in his career. 'I know now that I've met a lot of people with autism during my years on the job. I just didn't know it at the time.'

Advocates who become familiar with the needs of law enforcement and criminal justice professionals are better able to provide objective information to police and support for families who become involved in criminal justice situations. With appropriate planning and a firm commitment by a local organization, advocates can make a difference for their loved ones and their entire community.

12

Conclusion

My son, Kelly, is eighteen years old. He's now an adult who can make most of his own decisions. He's learning to drive and was able to obtain his learner's permit. He wants a job, a Dodge Ram pickup, and his own home. He wants to meet the right girl, get married, and maybe have children. Kelly, like most 18-year-olds, enjoys his independence. He likes to take walks, go to the store for the newspaper and sweets, and visit his friends in the neighborhood. Gay and I have worked hard as parents to open the world to him and to give him the best chance to achieve his independence. We see Kelly having the chance to realize his dreams. For this, we are very happy.

But we're frightened at the same time that we haven't done enough to prepare the world for Kelly. He still gets The Look from those who don't know him.

A police officer recently noticed Kelly when he went into the corner store recently to buy a dozen bottles of his favorite brand of orange juice while my wife waited in the car. He was merely stocking up so he wouldn't run out of his supply. When it comes close to running out, Kelly becomes very anxious that he will never get it again.

We're not sure what the officer saw that brought Kelly to his attention. Was it his unusual gait? His too cheerful manner? His loud tone of voice? Was it his body language combined with the fact that he was buying so much orange juice that attracted the officer's attention?

We don't know the reason, but the officer approached Kelly as he left the store and asked him if he had been drinking. Kelly said no. Our very resourceful son went on to explain his autism to the officer and produce his state picture identification card, an Autism Society of America laminated law enforcement awareness handout card that he carries, and my business card for law enforcement awareness workshops. He told the officer that the woman in the car was his mom. The officer told Kelly that he had attended one of my workshops for the Detroit Police Department and said to say hello to me. Everything worked out well for Kelly that day. But will this always be the case?

We worry that Kelly won't always know when and who to explain his autism to. We worry about his difficulty in knowing friend from foe. He told me recently that there are some kids on the next block who call him retard. I told him to ignore them and that he could always seek help from trusted neighbors and storeowners who know him. But we worry that, with the right approach, there are those who could manipulate him and his naiveté through a false friendship. We worry about what will happen when we are gone.

When one considers that autism-specific education for law enforcers did not exist until recently, these are in many ways boom times.

- Model curricula and videos have been produced.

- The law enforcement community is beginning to recognize autism issues in publications and training units.

- Legislation is being passed to ensure the continuity of law enforcement training to recognize those with autism and other developmental disabilities.

- Autism conferences and publications now feature presentations and articles about these issues.

- Information is being shared worldwide about this issue.

But this boom is the result of sole efforts by individuals who have come to recognize the importance of law enforcement awareness campaigns. These efforts are currently at the mercy of the time and energy that these individuals can devote. What's been missing is the organizational, lobbying, media, and credibility presence that national and international autism advocacy groups can bring to these endeavors. The materials, curricula, videos are only good when we use them effectively. To ensure their permanent use and to increase the profile of this information within the international law enforcement community, national and international autism advocacy organizations must become more involved.

A new generation of law enforcers will pass on the important lessons they learn early in their careers to the next generation of law enforcers, and so on. The new generation will become the supervisors and administrators of the future. As the autism population increases and matures, awareness among law enforcers should grow too. So it becomes even more important for advocates everywhere to establish permanent partnerships with these key members of the community. With our input, autism awareness can become standard training at academies for law enforcement and community service recruits.

Can we eliminate all unfortunate situations? No, but with mutual understanding, respect, and education we can make these predictable events become less severe and less frequent for our loved ones and improve their chances for fully independent, productive, and secure futures.

Resources

Curricula

Why Law Enforcement Needs to Recognize Autism
For requesting law enforcement agencies only. Use departmental letterhead:
Maryland Police and Correctional Training Commissions
3085 Hernwood Road
Woodstock, MD 21163–1099

Autism and Informed Response
Curriculum and video
South Carolina Autism Society
229 Parson Street 1-A
West Columbia, SC 29169

Video

Autism Awareness Video for Law Enforcement/Community Service Personnel
Autism Society of America 1–800–3-AUTISM or, contact author at ddpi@flash.net

Autism Society of North Carolina Bookstore
91974–0204
www.autismsociety.nc.org
919–743–0208
Fax: 919–743–0204
For orders outside the U.S. contact the author at ddpi@flash.net

Emergency Alert Window Decals

Autism Society of Illinois
2200 South Main Street, Suite 317
Lombard, IL 60148–5366
1–630–691–1270
www.autismillinois.org/decal.htm

Communications tracking technology

Global Positioning System (GPS)
Digital Angel Corporation
350 Motor Parkway, Suite 207
Hauppauge, NY 11788
1–631–951–3366
www.digitalangel.net

Radio Frequency (RF)
Care Trak
1031 Autumn Ridge Road
Carbondale, Illinois 62901
1–800–842–4537
www.caretrak.com

Cognitive visual aids
Police/Emergency Laminated Cards

Phrases for officer use in American Sign Language, symbols and words

KidAccess, Inc.
6256 Darlington Road
Pittsburgh, PA 16217
1–412–521–8552
www.kidaccess.com

ID jewelry

IdentiFind
5465 Dutch Cove Road
Canton, NC 28716–0567
1–828–648–6768
E-mail: labels@identifind.com

Advocacy organizations

Autism Society of America
7910 Woodmont Avenue, Suite 300
Bethesda, MD 20814–3067
1–800–3-AUTISM or 1–301–657–0881
www.autism-society.org

World Autism Organization
Avenue E. van Becelaere 26b (bte21)
1170 Brussels
Belgium
www.worldautism.org

Asperger's Syndrome Coalition of the United States, Inc.
P.O. Box 49267
Jacksonville Beach, FL 32240–9267
www.asperger.org

Online Asperger Syndrome Information and Support (OASIS)
www.aspergersyndrome.org

National Alliance for the Mentally Ill
Colonial Place Three
2107 Wilson Boulevard, Suite 300
Arlington, VA 22201
1–703–524–7600 or 1–800–950-NAMI
www.nami.org

The Arc
1–301–565–3842
www.thearc.org
www.thearc.org/ada/crim.html

Alzheimer's Association
919 North Michigan Avenue, Suite 1100
Chicago, IL 60611
1–800–272–3900
www.alz.org/caregiver/programs/safereturn.htm

To contact the author

Dennis Debbaudt
2338 S.E. Holland Street
Port Saint Lucie, FL 34952
561–398–9756
E-mail: ddpi@flash.net

References

Creedon, M. P., Debbaudt, D. and Campbell, M. (1996) 'Strategies For Safer Interaction within Communities.' In L.A. Tidey and J. Pequet (eds) *Open Minds Open Doors: Proceedings of the 1996 Autism Society of America National Conference.* Milwaukee, Wisconsin: Autism Society of America

Debbaudt, D. (1994) *Avoiding Unfortunate Situations: A Collection of Experiences, Tips and Information from and about People with Autism and Other Developmental Disabilities and Their Encounters with Law Enforcement Agencies.* Detroit, Michigan: Wayne County Society for Autistic Citizens (Way/SAC).

Debbaudt, D. (1996) *Educating the Public and Law Enforcement. A Handout for the Detroit-Wayne County Community Mental Health Agency Law Enforcement Training Workshop Series.* Detroit, MI: D-WCCMHA.

Debbaudt, D. (2000a) 'Avoiding Unfortunate Situations.' *The Source, A Publication of ASPEN of America, Inc.* Winter 2000, 3 and 6.

Debbaudt, D. (2000b) 'Law Enforcement Awareness of Autism: In Memory of Calvin Champion Jr.' *TASH Newsletter, 26,* 8, 30–32.

Debbaudt, D. (2001) 'You Do Not Have the Right To Remain Silent! A Report on Advocacy Efforts for Law Enforcement Professionals' Awareness of Autism.' *Autism Asperger's Digest Magazine,* January-February 2001, 22, 23 and 25.

Debbaudt, D. and Rothman, D. (2001) 'Contact With Individuals With Autism: Effective Resolutions.' *FBI Law Enforcement Bulletin, 7,* 4, 20–24.

Eugene Oregon Police Department (2000) *Special Needs Awareness Program (SNAP).* http://www.ci.eugene.or.us/dps/police/crime%20prevention/SNAP.htm

Farrar, P. (1996) *End the Silence: Preventing the Sexual Assault of Women with Communication Difficulties: Developing a Community Response.* Calgary, Alberta: The Technical Resource Centre.

Farrar, P. (1998) 'Preparing for the Interview.' In L. Hutchinson MacLean (ed) *Admissible In Court: Interviewing Witnesses Who Live With Disabilities.* Lethridge, Alberta, Canada: Hutchinson MacLean Productions.

Hildebrandt, M. (1993) 'Characteristics of a high-functioning autistic: The autistic triad.' In J.I. Adams (ed) *Autism and Pervasive Developmental Disorder: Creative Ideas During the School Years.* Kent Bridge, Ontario: Adams Publishers.

Hutchinson MacLean, L. (1998) *Admissible in Court: Interviewing witnesses who live with disabilities.* Lethbridge, Alberta: Hutchinson MacLean Productions.

Inbau, F. E. and Reid, J. E. (1967). *Criminal Interrogations and Confessions,* Baltimore, Maryland: Williams and Wilkins.

Little, L. (2000) 'Peer victimization of Children with AS and NLD.' *The Source, A Publication of the Asperger Syndrome Coalition of the United States, Inc.* Fall 2000.

Lord, W.D., Boudreaux, M.C. and Lanning, K.V. (2001) 'Investigating Potential Child Abduction Cases: A Developmental Perspective.' *FBI Law Enforcement Bulletin, 7,* 4, 1–10.

Moreno, S.J. (1991) *High Functioning Individuals With Autism: Advice and Information for Parents and Others Who Care.* Crown Point, Indiana: MaaP Services, Inc.

MPCTC (1999) *Why Law Enforcement Needs To Recognize Autism.* Woodstock, MD: Maryland Police and Correctional Training Commissions.

National Alliance for the Mentally Ill (1997) *Florida Establishes 'Mental Health' Court.* Press release. Arlington, VA: NAMI.

Perske, R. (1991) *Unequal Justice? What Can Happen When Persons With Developmental Disabilities Encounter the Criminal Justice System.* Nashville, Tennessee: Abingdon Press.

Petersilia, J. (2000) 'Doing Justice: Criminal Offenders with Developmental Disabilities.' *TASH Newsletter, 26,* 8, 11.

Schaeffer, P. (1998) 'Church watches as Dallas diocese regroups.' *National Catholic Reporter,* December 4, 1998.

Swift, J. (1998) *Autism Awareness Video for Law Enforcement / Community Service Personnel.* Harrisburg, PA: Autism Society of America.

United States Department of Education (2000) *Joint OCR/OSERS Letter on Disability Based Harassment.* Washington, DC: U.S. Department of Education. www.edlaw.net/service/harassment-disab.html

Subject Index

abduction, danger of, 81
abuse:
    in adult care industry, 53, 54
    allegations of, investigating,
        54–56
    identifying situations of, 51–54
    persons with autism as targets of,
        34, 50–59
    sexual, of persons with autism,
        53–54
    see also harassment, disability;
        schools, bullying in;
        victimization
Acquired Aphasia with Epilepsy or
    Landau–Kleffner Syndrome
    (LKS), 17
adult care industry, abuse in, 53, 54
advocates, autism, 104–127
aggressive behavior, 19, 20, 24, 27,
    37, 92–94, 111
Alliance for the Mentally Ill (AMI),
    123
Alzheimer's disease, 37, 38, 41, 42,
    77, 115, 123, 124
animals, reaction to, 19, 22, 25, 37,
    83, 88, 119, 122
Asperger's Syndrome, 17, 22, 33, 92,
    107, 108
assistance, calls for, 21–23, 28
asthma, 19, 26, 27, 88
authority figures, relationship with,
    46–47

autism (*passim*):
    advocacy organizations, role of,
        113–114, 130
    awareness training/campaigns, 14,
        106, 113–127
    behaviors indicative of, 17–22,
        116, 118–121
    biological determination of autism,
        16
    cognitive skills in, 17, 28, 110
    definition, 16–17
    incidence of, 16, 62
    information card, 19, 26, 101,
        102, 119
    levels of functioning in, 17
    recognition of, 17–22, 116,
        118–121
    response methodology, 28–30,
        121–122
Autism Society of America, 42, 43,
    60, 61, 76, 82, 105, 117, 125,
    126
    Advocate newsletter, 73
    Excellence in Media award, 125
    law enforcement awareness
        handout card, 125
Autism Spectrum Disorder (ASD),
    definition, 17
awareness, disability, 123
    autism-specific, 14, 70, 72,
        78–82, 85–86, 124–126
    for emergency and law
        enforcement agencies,
        39–43, 60–61, 63, 73,
        86, 89–90, 91–127, 129

Name Index